TO BE
AT
HOME

TO BE AT HOME

Christianity, Civil Religion, and World Community

Leroy S. Rouner

BEACON PRESS
Boston

Beacon Press
25 Beacon Street
Boston, Massachusetts 02108

Beacon Press books
are published under the auspices of
the Unitarian Universalist Association of Congregations.

98 97 96 95 94 93 92 91   8 7 6 5 4 3 2 1

Text design by Hunter Graphics

Library of Congress Cataloging-in-Publication Data

Rouner, Leroy S.
  To be at home : Christianity, civil religion, and world community
/ Leroy S. Rouner.
    p. cm.
  Includes bibliographical references and index.
  ISBN 0-8070-1016-2
  1. Christianity and international affairs. 2. Christianity and
culture. 3. Religious pluralism—Christianity.
  4. Christianity—20th century. 5. Civil religion. 6. Christianity
and other religions. I. Title.
  BR115.I7R68   1991
  261'.1—dc20   90-20822
                                                          CIP

For Timothy

You shall go out in joy,
and be led forth in peace;
the mountains and the hills before you
shall break forth into singing,
and all the trees of the field shall clap their hands.

Isaiah 55:12

Acknowledgments

Many have helped with this book. John Bennett, Peter Berger, Jim Heaney, Jim Langford, Paul Minear, Jürgen Moltmann, and Timothy Rouner have all read and commented on earlier drafts. No one, however, has been more helpful than my friend and mentor Robert McAfee Brown, who has read two versions and commented extensively on each. He was godfather to our son Timothy, so the care and critical sensitivity of his help with this book knits a close bond even more closely.

Bettina Bergo, my teaching assistant at Boston University, prepared the notes and index; Ted Gaiser typed an earlier version of the manuscript; and Barbara Darling-Smith, my administrative assistant at the Institute for Philosophy and Religion, copyedited the manuscript. No one has had more expert and congenial help in these areas, and to these three friends and colleagues I am more than grateful.

Deborah Johnson was not only my editor at Beacon Press; her instinctive enthusiasm for the theme, the detailed and sympathetic attention she gave to the manuscript, and the warmth she brought to this collegial adventure, have been gifts of friendship. I'm glad I know her. And while the book is not all that it might be, it is a whole lot better because of her work on it.

Finally, those who know Josiah Royce's book *The Problem of Christianity*, and Ernest Hocking's work *The Coming World Civilization*, will understand my debt to them both. I have not attempted to match their metaphysical depth. I have tried, rather, to show in practical and historical terms how part of the problem of Christianity actually works itself out in the coming world civilization.

Contents

Introduction

WHAT contribution can Christianity make to a world community where people of different religions and cultures can be at home? And how can that contribution be made without either excluding others or compromising Christian faith?

The human future depends on developing some measure of human community, because the major issues of politics and health—world peace and ecological protection—are global problems. Even with the end of the Cold War, the continuing spread of nuclear weapons and the increasing threat of serious ecological damage require a measure of international cooperation that was heretofore thought impossible. That cooperation will not be reliable if it is built on fear alone. It will be reliable only when various peoples come to claim these issues as common problems because they understand themselves to be part of a common people.

The great world religions have historically been major forces in shaping a community sense of being at home in our world. They have provided a sense of who we are, why we are here, and what we need to do so that our lives can be whole and worthwhile. Religions have regularly been at odds with one another, however, especially in the West. To be a Christian has too often meant to fight the Muslims, denigrate the Jews, and reject the religions of the Far East.

Contemporary interreligious conversation finds many Christians eager to make amends by celebrating the virtues of those religious communities that they previously scorned. Whether from guilt or the delights of discovery, Christian participants in this dialogue have sometimes been better at appreciating the other person's faith than they have been at professing their own. I continue to learn much from other religious traditions, but my agenda here is how I can best share with others what gladdens my heart and persuades my spirit in matters of religious faith. The purpose of this book, therefore, is to explore the Christian experience of community building and to show how it is relevant to the larger human community.

We all need to find a way to live with our differences, and Christianity has something to offer to that need, as a result of its long history of struggle with the problem of community. That struggle began with those ancient tribes that came to-gether to form Israel, and it gradually evolved into an affir-mation about the universality of humankind. Christianity's idea of a universal human community was eventually threat-ened, however, by the breakdown of Christian culture at the close of the European Middle Ages and the subsequent plu-ralism of a modern culture dominated increasingly by indi-vidualism, rationalism, and secularism.

From the early seventeenth century onward, modern Christianity was no longer the direct and determinative cul-tural authority it had been in the High Middle Ages. If it was to have any cultural influence at all on those modern individ-uals and institutions which were no longer Christian, that influence would now have to be indirect and generalized, ap-pealing to the merits of Christian insight as its only power of persuasion. The Christian idea of a universal human com-munity would have to be freed from dogmatism and exclu-sivism, as well as its Western cultural orientation, in order to join with other living traditions of belief, both religious and secular, which also sought a universal human community. The challenge was to do this without forfeiting the integrity of the Christian affirmation.

The relation to democracy was a particularly significant part of the Christian response to modern secularism. Not all Christians were democrats in the early years of the modern experiment with popular rule, but democracy was clearly the political development that best served the Christian commitment to community. Democracy announced that each individual had an inherent human value that bestowed certain inalienable rights and required equality before the law. This secular political philosophy was consonant with St. Paul's theological announcement, in his letter to the church in Galatia, that "there is neither Jew nor Greek, there is neither slave nor free, there is neither male nor female; for you are all one in Christ Jesus" (Gal. 3:28).

Through indirect relationships such as its growing support for democracy, Christianity became a major contributor to the "civil religion" of some democratic societies. This civil religion was the self-defining creed whereby people of different religious, ethnic, and ideological backgrounds understood themselves as a common people with a common national purpose. Without the common sense of identity, loyalty, and purpose provided by civil religion, the individualism and rationalism of modern pluralistic society would have made democracy dysfunctional, for there would have been no common ground. Civil religion, for example, makes possible the paradox of a "loyal opposition" within a national government. It is the binding ingredient of a pluralistic democracy, holding individuals and institutions to the national community even when their particular political will has not prevailed.

From the Christian theological point of view, alliances with secular individuals and institutions serve the work of God's Kingdom. That is not what secular or non-Christian people understand themselves to be doing, however, so Christian thought struggles to balance its own conviction about the universal human community with respect and acceptance of others' convictions.

After a generation of missionary endeavor that has too often been imperial and imperious, the winsome virtues of "a still, small voice" rather than a loud, aggressive one are increasingly apparent. The conversation among people of differing religious and cultural traditions must be an occasion for making friends, not conquering enemies; and the appropriate approach to a friend is to say, in effect, "This is my experience; is it yours also? Does it have something of our common humanity in it?" That is the kind of conversation which I have tried to advocate and emulate.

Part One begins with the original development of the Christian idea of community, from the struggle over tribalism among the ancient Israelites to the potential universalism of Paul's vision of a Christian community in which Jews and Greeks, slaves and free, male and female would all be one. Tribal bonds were the natural bonds of blood, region, language, caste or class, and cultic "religion." Paul's view of the human community was not tribal, or cultic, or "religious" in this sense. The new bond was faith in the Creator God who both transcended creation and was incarnate in it in Jesus, who inaugurated a new human community. That community overcame distinctions among the natural bonds of tribal groups.

After Jesus' death and resurrection the little Christian community anticipated the end of the world in a matter of months. When this did not happen, Christianity needed a new understanding of how God was at work in history to bring in the Kingdom. God's work was now understood to include both the Christian community and the surrounding non-Christian world, so Part One concludes with a discussion of Augustine's *City of God*, the first major Christian exploration of inter- and intracultural conflict, and the first developed philosophical argument that the God of the Christians is at work outside the Christian church as well as within it. Part One also introduces the conflict between individualism and community, which becomes critical in the modern world and is an important theme in Part Two.

Part Two explores the challenge of modern secularism, rationalism, and individualism to the Christian idea of community and the ways in which the Christian idea of community became relevant in a pluralistic society. The focus is on nations as communities, rather than on those cultural groups within nations where we admittedly have our strongest and most intimate bonds with others. Modern nations are abstract entities, and the nature of the national cause is inevitably vague. However, nations are significant for a philosophy of community, precisely because they force the community issue, as in the current ethnic conflicts in the Soviet Union.

Those conflicts remind us that traditional, tribal or ethnic identity is a major source of social and political conflict. The American political debate over the forces that make for world peace and community previously neglected this point. The American debate focused on economy. The Right emphasized capitalism and anticommunism, while the Left argued for economic justice as keys to peace and world community. But the newly emerging ethnic movements are only secondarily driven by economic interest, whether capitalist, communist, or of the liberal/social justice variety. In Soviet Azerbaijan, for example, the "prodemocracy" movement is really a call for traditional ethnic solidarity, not a forward move toward modern democratic freedoms. It is a rejection of identity in a larger community with those of different ethnic backgrounds. That rejection is stimulated by economic hardship and political injustice, but the driving force is the desire of an ethnic group for the independent right to decide its polity primarily in terms of its ethnicity. "Ethnocracy" is the political goal. This "retribalization" of politics shows how strong ethnic identities are, even after years of being submerged under "national" loyalties. The collapse of militant communist totalitarianism in Russia has ironically encouraged balkanization in the name of premodern values.

One can argue that nations like the Soviet Union and

China are too big to be cost-efficient anyway, and that balkanization—the political equivalent of a corporate shake-
out—will be initially painful, but eventually profitable. One
can even agree, as I do, with Stephen Toulmin who argues
that much of what modern nationalism has taught us in the
West now needs to be unlearned. Nevertheless, it is the entity
of the nation that holds our feet to the fire on the community
issue. Balkanization says, "Let's go home to our own people,
where we won't have to deal with strangers. In our ethnic
homeland we will all be the same, so we can trust each other,
and live in peace." But, of course, ethnic communalism never
lives in peace. Ethnocracies include their own kind only by
excluding some other kind, who never live very far away. And
having thus inevitably made enemies out of the strangers on
their borders, they are constantly fearful. And fear leads to a
fight: Sinhalese and Tamils in Sri Lanka; Catholics and Protestants in Ireland; Hindus and Muslims in the Indian subcontinent; Arabs and Israelis in the Middle East; the list is
endless.

This is not to endorse the simplistic view that all present
national boundaries are sacrosanct. On the contrary, we are
now entering a postcolonial, post–World War II period of
realignment in national boundaries, and justice is finally being
done in places like the Baltic states and other victims of colonialism. This is only right, and I support much of this realignment. I only mean to argue, somewhat paradoxically,
that the modern nation is the major maker of a universal
human community—in spite of the threat to that community
which nationalism represents—because it requires various
sorts and conditions of people to overcome at least some of
their instinctive and visceral alienation from one another. By
making ethnic groups live in terms of some minimal common
ground with one another, the nation becomes a school for
international and universal human community.

The prospect of a world community is dependent upon
the extent to which the nations that constitute a world
community have at least begun to solve their own internal

communal problems. There are admittedly numerous trans-national and transcultural organizations, institutions, and movements which affect world community for good or ill—multinational corporations, international terrorist groups, ecumenical religious bodies, and so forth—but the issue of world community and world peace needs the beginnings of a solution very soon. Some functional semblance of world community must be established in the next generation if we are to avoid nuclear catastrophe or ecological disaster. Americans have been so absorbed in the Cold War that its end is heralded as the coming of peace. But the superpower politics of the Cold War held the politics of ethnicity at bay. The Soviet Union is now threatened with civil war, and all the makings of civil strife are present in China. With the sophisticated international arms trade that has supplied groups as diverse as the Afghan rebels and the Tamil Tigers available to a growing number of near-fanatical ethnic conflicts, it is not clear that the end of the Cold War has actually brought world peace and universal human community closer. The nuclear threat from superpowers was muted by a measure of responsibility and an awareness of the enormous cost of nuclear war to each superpower. Nuclear weapons in the hands of ethnic terrorists are not under those restraints. The end of the Cold War brings new dangers. The urgency of human community building to ensure peace is, if anything, increased. And nations will surely continue to be the major players in the new politics of world peace.

The question then arises, What kind of nation in our present world is a congenial bearer of the Christian commitment to world community? Or, to put the question in Christian theological terms, Where is God at work in our current history, preparing for that great community which is the Kingdom of God?

Democracy, I suggest, is the political context in which world community is being shaped and God is at work. I do not know that democracy is the best of all possible political systems, but I am persuaded that it is the best of the presently available ones. I also believe that God is at work in other political contexts, in ways which I would find thoroughly surprising. Nevertheless, genuinely democratic societies incorporate commitment to the dignity of the individual human being, in spite of racial, religious, sexual, ethnic, and cultural differences. That inclusiveness is in keeping with Paul's vision of a community where fundamental differences would be overcome by loyalty to a common cause.

There are authoritarian regimes, however, that claim to be democracies but give only lip service to democratic ideals. I have used America and India as illustrations of two rather different ways in which Christianity has indirectly influenced ideas and values in genuine democracies.

America challenges the relevance of Christianity to a modern secular nation that celebrates rationalism and individualism. India challenges the relevance of Christianity to a religiously pluralistic nation. These two national challenges are paradigm cases for the critical issues of a world community.

America was an early large-scale, self-conscious experiment with democracy. India is a successor to the American experiment insofar as it deals with a much more complex set of cultural and religious conflicts than America has ever had to confront. India is unique not only because of the size of its diverse population and because of the fact that its democracy works with a largely illiterate electorate, but also because India shaped a constitution which, from the beginning, was committed to democratic values for a people of radical educational, linguistic, caste or class, cultural, and religious diversity.

In both cases the question is how Christianity can make its distinctive contribution to a culture without needing to capture that culture and make it "Christian." For the Christian contribution to be creative, however, it cannot be isolated, superficial, or minimal. That contribution must become a fundamental part of the deep structure of a nation's values, goals, and self-understanding. Otherwise it is only of incidental interest. I have referred to that deep structure as a nation's "civil religion" because, in both America and India, national goals, purposes, and values have been the substance of national identity.

Both have been what Carl Friedrich referred to as "creedal nations" rather than nations bound by natural cultural ties.[1] Friedrich's point was that a culturally pluralistic nation needs a creed of some sort to give its venture in nation building both purpose and identity. Since pluralism is a condition that a world community must accept and deal with, it is creedal nations which will show the way. Friedrich's civil "creed" is what I mean by civil "religion" and is not far from what Josiah Royce meant by the "loyalty" which made possible what he called "the Great Community."[2]

For Royce, of course, "community" was a metaphysical reality. I have not tried to argue that case here, since it would require a separate book, although I have indicated briefly in the chapter entitled "Modern Homelessness and the Individual" how metaphysical loneliness has made the issue of community so compelling.

Democracy in both America and India is peculiarly vulnerable because of the communal conflicts that are built into the structure of national life. Each nation celebrates pluralism and cultural diversity, so each illustrates the need that is vital for a world community. That need is for some deeply felt common bond that can at least make the national community workable, since the great mystery of an honest democracy is what holds it together. If I object strongly to the opposition's candidate, which I confess I regularly do, why should I claim him as my president when he wins, as, alas, he regularly does? Why should I be loyal to majority rule when the majority seems to me to rule so badly? The bond that holds me in community with my recalcitrant compatriots is not some weak national consensus, since that would not explain my curious behavior. In order to survive the external threats that most democratic nations now face—not to mention the inner despair of that 49 percent of the citizenry who are regular losers in any national referendum—there must be a profoundly held, overriding sense of national value and purpose which persuades most of the populace, for most of the time, that this is a good place to be, and that this national venture is a good thing to be doing together, even if the leadership is not of one's own choosing.

That persuasion is at the heart of civil religion. It is more than patriotism because it presupposes that these goals and purposes have some universal value, a presupposition which gives them their creative power. In this sense the nation is not just a larger tribe, because its self-identifying civil religion is not intended to exclude anyone. America celebrates a civil religion of freedom and calls it "the American way." India celebrates a civil religion of tolerance and says, "This is our Indian custom." In neither case is the claim for freedom or tolerance exclusively American or Indian. Because of their particular history and cultural development, we can learn something distinctive about freedom from the Americans, and something distinctive about tolerance from the Indians, but freedom and tolerance are universal human values. Civil religion at its best is therefore an opening out toward world community. And it is in contributing to that civil religion in both America and India that Christian ideas and values have actually become effective, without being either imperialistic or concessionist. They have maintained their integrity and, at the same time, have been freely adopted by the larger community.

When this indirect contribution to a non-Christian culture's self-understanding happens creatively, it represents the Christian ethic of "losing one's life" in order to find it; of giving away one's insight and values to one's neighbors without needing to cling to the institutional claim that they are "Christian." This ethic "finds its life" in serving God's purposes in a way that would have been impossible had it insisted on maintaining its institutional Christian claim. For if the Christian vision of a world community is to be fulfilled, it will necessarily be mostly non-Christian people who make it happen.

But civil religion admittedly has been regularly destructive. When institutional religious claims—like those made by the American Moral Majority or the PTL Club—are made on a nation's civil religion, as they have been so often, the result is disastrous, both for the nation and the religious community. The corruption of civil religion in America by Protestant evangelical groups is a recent example. Even more serious have been the corruptions of civil religion in Nazi Germany and currently in Iran, where millions died because of a zealous idolization of the nation, which corrupted both religion and the state.

Civil religion is democracy's precious bane. It is a constant thorn in the flesh of the body politic, but it is a necessary element in any pluralistic, democratic society that seeks to bring its people together in the service of a common cause.

The remaining question for Part Three is a methodological one. Has the aggressiveness of some Christian evangelism been a misuse of power? I think it has. Christians have too often used the Christian message to gain power over others, whereas the spirit of "losing one's life" for the neighbor is one of conferring power *on* others. We need to learn to think in this new way of conferring power *on* others if the Christian message is to be free from the corruption of power seeking.

That message is an offering, not an argument, an appeal rather than an attack. Trusting that truth has its own power, true believers will be content to speak softly in confessing their Christian conviction. Speaking in this new way becomes possible when we have overcome our fear of the other.

In the end I come full circle, back to the traditional bonds of blood, region, land, language, caste or class, and religion, the original communal bonds with which Christianity struggled, and which have been so divisive in the quest for a genuinely human community. They nevertheless persist, in spite of modern individualism.

The blood bond is the most fundamental of these. What we need today is a new notion of the blood bond as universally human. What we have in common is the fact that we are all part of the human race. The symbol of this new racial awareness is a gift of modern technology—a picture of planet Earth from the moon. The astronauts who took the picture were, at that moment, thinking of the whole Earth as home and of themselves as representing humankind in their space venture. This new notion of the old blood bond helps make a world community possible.

Christianity and *Christian* are broad and complex realities. My reference is to a minimal classic core of belief and commitment that most Christian people hold in common. An adequate defense of that claim would require more space than this book allows, so I must beg the reader's empathy. My particular tradition within Christianity is Protestant and Congregational, which is to say that I regard Christianity essentially as a movement, not as an institution, a movement defined by biblical faith and faithful life, not by ecclesiastical hierarchy or traditional authority.

The book is dedicated to my son Timothy, who died in 1977 at the age of nineteen while climbing with his older brother, Rains, attempting a first ascent of the northwest face of Devil's Thumb, near Petersburg, Alaska.[3]

Tim read an earlier version of this book, and he and I had several conversations about its general thesis. He would come into the study in the evening and sit in the leather wingback chair in the corner with his long legs stretching out beyond the fireplace into the middle of the room. When horsing around in the kitchen, or at family mealtime, he would laugh a lot. In the study, however, he was serious and intense.

During his senior year at the White Mountain School in Littleton, New Hampshire, he had written a thesis on secondary education called "Too Much Success, Not Enough Happiness." He was a good writer, and a rapidly developing poet. He cared about what happened to people; he remembered India, where he had lived as a child; and he was intrigued by the way I was trying to put together my experience of India with my experience as an American and my commitment as a Christian.

At a time when I was fumbling with a disparate set of new ideas, Tim was more interested and encouraging than anyone else. So my dedication of the book to him is not just a father's cherishing of his lost son. It is an honest memorandum of a debt owed to one who understood me, and helped me.

> High Meadow Farm
> North Sandwich,
> New Hampshire

Part I

1

Christianity and Tribalism

THE Old Testament understanding of community centers on the idea of the people of God who are formed out of different tribes into a new nation, Israel, by means of a covenant with God. This covenant transforms the natural bonds of land, blood, language, caste or class, and religious ritual, which are the communal bonds of tribal or traditional societies. This Judeo-Christian encounter with tribalism thus initiates a new understanding of what a community is.

The Hebrew Bible—the Christian Old Testament—views God as transcendent over the world. This view stood in sharp contrast to the nature religions of the communities around Israel. In the religions of Canaan, for example, gods and goddesses were tribal powers and were worshipped because they were believed to control natural forces such as wind and rain, and historic forces of tribal destiny, such as prosperity and peace. They were as numerous as the tribes they served and the natural forces that beset them. For Israel, however, there was one God who was revealed through natural forces and historic events, but who was always Lord over them.

There are several Old Testament accounts of Israel's covenant with God, but they all have common features. Typical is the covenant narrative in the twenty-fourth chapter of the Book of Joshua. Here God chooses Israel and confirms this election in a historical succession of "mighty acts" whereby God leads the Israelites through the wilderness, feeds them with manna from heaven, chastises them for their wickedness, and yet forgives them, delivers them from bondage in Egypt, is their champion in battle with their enemies, and brings them finally to the Promised Land.

In the act of convenanting, the tribes agree to become a new community, "the people of God." In so doing, they discover a new source of their identity as a people. Formerly the tribe had understood common identity through natural bonds of region, blood, language, caste or class, and religious ritual. The tribal gods—"the gods your fathers served in the region beyond the river"—were personifications of these natural identities.[1] Now a tribal people gives up these natural identities for a new loyalty to a transcendent God.

Israel knew God as revealed in the midst of historical events. God was not so much a power in nature as an actor in history. Israel trusted that God had chosen Israel and would lead the people to the "promised land" of Canaan. Even when Israel went astray, or fell into bondage in Egypt, God remained faithful, and after many years of wandering in the wilderness, God provided the gift of the Promised Land.

This promise of land is Israel's central hope, and this promise becomes the symbol around which many of the critical themes of Israel's life are gathered. Yahweh is known as the God of the Promise. For a nomadic people, the promise of a rich land flowing with milk and honey where they could live a secure and settled life was a naturally appealing dream. Israel sought both freedom from bondage in Egypt and deliverance from precarious wandering in the desert. Weary of being a bird of passage, Israel yearned for a place where security and freedom could meet. The great religious heroes of these people were all celebrated for the part they played in bringing Israel home to the Promised Land. This yearning for a place to be, and the faith that God would provide it, is the earliest and most fundamental element in Israel's creed.

In the theology of the Old Testament, therefore, the promise of land is evidence that God is active in history. The god of the land is no longer the power of the land as primal life force but the giver and redeemer of the life force itself. This belief did not derive from philosophical speculation, or a mythological imagination, but from the experience of God's acts in history. And this experience of a transcendent God who was nevertheless in its midst gave Israel a new understanding of God's immanence.

In tribal religion, the presence and power of gods and goddesses is a symbolization of the life force inherent in natural and historical events. The divinity of these powers is the experienced mystery of the life force itself. These life-force divinities are the meaning of the event, because they are its inherent power. They are, so to speak, the eventfulness of the event: the forcefulness of the wind, the torrentiality of the rain, the awesomeness of darkness, the inexplicability of death. Primal tribal religion has its beginnings, then, in this fundamental experience of life as power and mystery. It is humankind paying its respects to the daemonic, the primal life force.

Israel, as God's covenant people, did not stop believing in tribal gods. Life was still mysterious, and while Yahweh now also worked through flood and fire, he did not entirely dispossess the tribal world powers. God was present with Israel, not as the inherent mystery at the heart of things, but as Lord over that mystery, even while participating in the historic process.

God's immanence now meant that God joined Israel's historic life as personal Lord of a human community, one who was not subject to daemonic powers but rather made his people subject to him. He was the "Lord of lords." The covenant with Israel insists that other gods be subject to Yahweh: "Thou shalt have no other gods before me." To worship any of the other gods as the One Transcendent Holy World Power became both false and faithless.

A second critical dimension of God's promise to Israel concerned the blood bond, and the transformation of tribal blood bonds in the story of Israel is symbolized by the epic in which God promises a child to Abraham and Sarah.

Abraham trusted God, yet he knew that both he and his wife were too old to have children, so a note of anxious perplexity sounds faintly in the background of his story even as Abraham sings songs of praise to Yahweh for his faithfulness. Abraham becomes rich with cattle and silver and gold, and God repeats the promise: "I will make your descendants as the dust of the earth; so that if one can count the dust of the earth, your descendants also can be counted."[2] But Abraham's wife, Sarah, is barren, and Abraham continues to grow old. Finally God fulfills the promise to Abraham, and his son Isaac is born in Abraham's old age. But God claims Isaac as a sacrifice to test Abraham's faith. Abraham shows his willingness to make his only son a burnt offering to God, because God has called him. As a result, God stays the hand of Abraham as he takes the knife to kill Isaac.

This transformation of the blood bond is symbolized for Israel in a renewal of the covenant between God and Abraham, in which God gives both Abraham and Sarah new names, and in which he establishes a new sign of the covenant, circumcision. While not uniquely an Israelite practice, circumcision eventually became the major symbol for Israel that its tribal life was now in a new context, and that the procreation of the blood line was itself invaded by God's covenanting commandments.

Language and class status are the other traditional bonds with which we are concerned. They were interrelated issues for Israel. The matter of language features briefly but dramatically in the myth of the tower of Babel, an early attempt to explain the diversity of human tongues.[3] Diversity is a curse, because it makes it impossible for diverse peoples to understand one another. For Israel, language was a key element in religious life, for Israel understood its relation to God in terms of call, commandment, covenant, and Word. The God of Israel is a God who speaks. In spite of the importance of the cult and the role of the priest, the most definitive and original role in Israel's religious life is that of the prophet, the one who speaks for God.

Israel's attitude toward class and caste is both remarkable and revealing. Israelites saw themselves in the role of the alien, enslaved, wandering people who had no claim on this promised land which now identified them, the place where they belonged. The laws of Deuteronomy made clear that the people of Israel in the Promised Land were to remember their wandering in the desert, lest they forget that the Promised Land was God's, given to Israel in sacred trust. Israel's vocation in this new settlement was to remember what it had been like to be "a stranger and a sojourner" and to be neighbor to strangers, the fatherless, and the widow, remembering that Israel was a people without status.

"You shall not pervert the justice due to the sojourner or the fatherless, or take a widow's garment in pledge; but you shall remember that you were a slave in Egypt and the Lord your God redeemed you from there; therefore I command you to do this."[4] Strangers were to have a portion of each household's yearly income, as a tithe to the Lord. In this way, the inheritors of the Promised Land remembered those who had no home.

The New Testament is focused on the reality of God as incarnate in Jesus, the Christ. This view represents a radical development of Israel's religious insight and stands over against the Hellenistic religions of the Roman Empire with which the New Testament community in Palestine was surrounded. New Testament theology is a development of Israel's religious insight insofar as it is the fulfillment of the Old Testament prophecy of the Messiah, the Suffering Servant who would redeem Israel. It is a radical view, however, insofar as it announces a kingdom which is not of this world, established in the person and work of one who is himself the Son of God.

It is distinct from the religions of Hellenism, because it insists on a philosophical paradox that to Hellenistic thinking was incomprehensible. That paradox was the view that the universal, transcendent reality of God has become a finite, particular person in history.[5] It rejects the gnostic presupposition of much Hellenistic religion that religious salvation comes through the realization of a divine knowledge. It believes rather that salvation comes through participation in Christ, by which it means sharing the mind of Christ and becoming part of the body of Christ. New Testament theology seeks to establish a new understanding of community—for which neither the philosophical insight of Hellenism into the divine Logos nor the religious insight of Israel into the divine transcendence was entirely adequate.

The New Testament view of community was rooted in the prophetic tradition of Israel, in which the Kingdom of God always transcended the kingdoms of this world. This newly emerging idea of a Christian community emphasized the intimate, equal human relations with the poor, the outcast, and the oppressed, which became the stuff of Christian ethics. Hellenism's culture of the Roman gentleman was masculine, aristocratic, and hierarchical, whereas the newly emerging fellowship of Christians emphasized equality.

Roman Hellenism shared with Christianity a creative insight into monotheism, and the early Christians learned a good deal from Hellenism, especially its universalism and ethical idealism. But Roman religion made gods of their political leaders, thereby reviving a form of the old primal nature religion and its fundamental sin, idolatry. So the Christian reinterpretation of those natural, tribal bonds of blood, region, language, caste and class, and religion, in shaping a new understanding of community, drew much more heavily on their Jewish past than on the Hellenistic world of their present.

That Jewish past was reshaped in fundamental ways, however. In dealing with the blood bond, for example, the familial genealogy plays as important a role in the New Testament as it does in the Old. Matthew's gospel emphasizes the fact that Jesus of Nazareth was of the house of David through a specific, extensive genealogy. And at the heart of this blood-bond consciousness was the symbol of circumcision. Circumcision had been the mark of Israel's faith, the definitive sign of Israelitic culture and religion, and it loomed large in the thinking of those Jews who formed the early Christian community.

For Israel the clear distinction between Yahweh and all other gods, the definite requirements of the Law, and the ritual acts of moral and spiritual purification were all of a piece. Israel symbolized this coherent self-understanding in circumcision. So it is difficult to overemphasize the significance of the conflict over circumcision that developed between Paul and the so-called "Judaizers" in the early Christian community, but it is easy to misinterpret what was at stake.[6]

Peter, when he represented the Judaizers' concern, was not seeking to exclude Gentiles from the church. God's covenant was potentially with "all the peoples" and the Gentiles were to be welcomed. Nor had the high religion of Israel understood circumcision in a clumsy or primitive way, as a ritual with inherent power to identify the circumcised one with the covenant community. Its most profound understanding of circumcision had been symbolic, not primitively magical. The physical change in the genital organ represented a spiritual change in the heart of the man. There are numerous Old Testament references to the wicked as those with "uncircumcised hearts."[7] Even Paul, whose refusal to require physical circumcision of Gentile converts had initiated the crisis in the early church, spoke approvingly of circumcision in this symbolic sense.

But Paul believed that this blood-related symbol should not be mistaken for participation in the new community in Christ, for then the community would be limited to those identified with that blood line. Paul wanted a potentially universal community, and his view finally prevailed in the early church. For first-century Judaism, especially the religious officialdom of Pharisees, scribes, and elders, oneness with the Holy was tied to observance of the Law, the rite of circumcision, temple worship, Scripture, tradition, and the appointed religious authorities. The followers of Jesus respected most of these, but sought to reinterpret them.

Their principle of reinterpretation was that the grace of

God had transcended the Law. This was why Jesus had violated the Law of the sabbath by feeding his disciples with corn plucked on the holy day, and healing the sick.[8] These actions violated the letter of the Law, but not, as he understood it, the spirit. The essential sense of alienation between one person and another, inherent in the idea that some things are unclean, was not dismissed in a cavalier manner. There are indeed critical issues of alienation that must be faced and fought. But Jesus had insisted that they are not ritual issues, or legal matters, or traditional practices.

It is not unclean to eat meat offered to idols, Paul insisted. It is not unclean to work at healing the sick or feeding the hungry on the sabbath day, Jesus insisted. It is not unclean to baptize Gentiles who are uncircumcised, Peter finally insisted. What is unclean, they all insisted, is to fail in love for one's neighbor.

The centrality of love for the neighbor was the distinguishing feature of the early Christian community and marked a radical break with all forms of tribalism. This new Christian affirmation focused on the person and work of Jesus, the Christ. He was "Christ for me," as Dietrich Bonhoeffer was later to call him, and whatever Christianity had to offer that was distinctive and helpful was from him.[9]

2

The Christian Affirmation

JESUS has had a wide human appeal and has been a major ethical role model for the human community. But the idea that the man Jesus was somehow God incarnate in a fully human life has bemused and offended many people. Some reply that we are all divine and have the spirit of God in us, so Jesus is not essentially different from ourselves. Others recognize a very high degree of moral achievement in Jesus and think of him as an ethical exemplar. Still others have thought of Jesus as one of several great teachers and prophets in the world's religious history, each with a special gift for a particular place and time. Confucius, Gautama, Moses, Jesus, Mohammed, Gandhi—all have been religious spirits of unusual sensitivity and charisma, capable of formulating an ethical vision with profound simplicity.

Because the Christian claim that Jesus was both human and divine in a unique sense has been associated with Christian exclusivism, most people reject it. It seems an unlikely basis for an inclusive human community, but this paradoxical claim about Jesus is at the heart of Christianity's understanding of a genuinely human community.

The New Testament church—"the new community in Christ"—was not a group who gathered because of Jesus' charisma, or moral example, or intellectual capacities as a spiritual teacher. The members of the new community felt themselves bound together by the reality of God, which they had experienced in and through the presence of the man Jesus. One cannot prove that such an experience is really an experience of God. The revelation that Jesus is both human and divine comes to those who see him with "eyes of faith." This kind of knowing is not primarily empirical or logical; nor is it *realization* in the Hindu or Buddhist sense of suddenly grasping a point of view that one had not previously been able to comprehend. In *realization* one is confronted with a mystic vision of reality that is self-confirming, convincing one of the reality of God and the wisdom of certain truths about God.

Revelation, in the Christian understanding, is different from the *realization* of Hinduism and Buddhism. It is not an insight given to an isolated individual. It is a moment of individual participation in the community of those who live the historic events of Jesus' life and death and resurrection with him. The means of this participation is the story of those events, the testimony or testament to them. Revelation is reading that story as one's own story—the story of my Lord and my community of faith—and participating in that gathering of people who understand their life together to be a continuation of the story about Jesus and his people. In the same way that one knows one is loved by another only through living one's relationship to that person, never being able to point to any specific fact which absolutely establishes the certainty that one is loved, so the knowledge that Jesus is both God and man is the result of lived relationship to his story.

The event that creates the New Testament community is the resurrection of Jesus. During his lifetime there had been a group of those who followed, trusted, and believed in him. At his death, however, this group was dispersed. Even the faithful Peter, who had been most emphatic in his devotion and had been most convinced that Jesus was, indeed, the Christ, had denied Jesus and fled. "The New Testament com-

munity" refers to those like Peter and James and John, who
were with Jesus before his crucifixion and who had been
through the heady days of discipleship, the anxiety of the last
week in Jerusalem, the cataclysmic events of Gethsemane,
Jesus' arrest and trial, and the final crushing defeat of his
death.

That group was destroyed by his death. They had understood him in different ways, mostly the ways in which people
today still hold him in high regard. They thought of him as
a moral exemplar, a spiritual guru, a charismatic leader, a
religious teacher. They had been troubled by the thought that
perhaps he was more than that. Some said he was Messiah,
the Christ, the One who was to come. But how could they
know that? When he died their identity as a group died with
him, and their identification of him as moral leader, guru, and
teacher also died. For these functions they needed him in the
flesh, and with his death on the cross that possibility was
gone. The event of the resurrection did not restore Jesus to
the old community of his followers, but some of those who
had trusted and believed in him saw him again in the resurrected body.

It was not a vision or apparition of Jesus. The narratives
describe his body and manner as different enough so that he
was not immediately recognizable. At the same time, the resurrected Jesus was not bodiless. The narratives are full of
physical detail; people touched him, saw his wounds, heard
him speak. He was present only briefly, however; there was
no sense that he had simply returned to life as in the miracle
of the raising of Lazarus. What the resurrection appearances
did for the old community of Jesus' followers was to recon-
stitute them as a new community.

The idea that Jesus was somehow God incarnate was a
later formulation of the experience of those who had known
him "in the flesh," had suffered through the events of his
death, and had found in his resurrection appearances a tangible, historical event through which they could see what previously they had not been able to see. The point for them was

not that God was a miracle worker, who brought life out of death the way dead seeds produce new plants in the spring. They all knew about springtime, and they all had always believed in a general resurrection of the dead at the end of time. Neither of these popular beliefs could have produced the miracle of a community whose faith in Jesus as the Christ was now unshakable, even in the face of Peter's death, the imprisonment and death of Paul, and the persecution of the church by Roman authority.

The community that gathered in Jesus' lifetime had been a community of followers. The new community was a community of participants. In a mystical and sacramental sense, they understood themselves to constitute the living body of the risen Lord. Previously they had been often perplexed, full of apprehensive questions, and easily defeated. After the resurrection they spoke with authority, were confident in their proclamation of the good news, and were steadfast, even when confronting Roman power. Participation in this new community was still an act of individual will, but the radical nature of the community's life—such as the practice of sharing all things—was made possible by the conviction that the Holy Spirit of God had descended upon them. They felt themselves gifted with a new power. Their participation in the body of the new community, which had been brought into being by Jesus' resurrection and could therefore rightly be called the body of the risen Christ, was a power to live in a new way and to do deeds of faithfulness.

These deeds ranged from acts of healing others to the sacrifice of their own lives for their faith. The enabling power behind these acts, however, they understood to be the power of God for salvation. They believed themselves to be saved from the powers of sin and death. Salvation from sin did not mean that they could do no moral wrong or that they ceased to be affected by "the power of sin." It meant that the power of sin to cause the death of final separation from God was broken. Through repentance and faith it was now possible to trust that God loved them in spite of their sinfulness—not just through the mind's belief that Jesus had been God with them, but through the continued experience of life in the body of those who had been constituted as a new community in him.

That the Christian cult did eventually spread throughout the world may be regarded either as an act of God, if one is a believer, or an accident of history, if one is not. There are Christians who argue that the spread of Christianity is empirical proof of God's intention, but this logic is readily shown to be flawed by the impressive spread of so much that God clearly abhors.

But did the early Christians intend to foster a new *humanity*, or is this idea only a later addendum, hastily affirmed now that a planetary world demands it? The answer to this question lies in the reality of Jesus, the Christ. What meaning for the future did he embody? What was the message of his life and work that the resurrection revealed as God's effective purpose in the world?

Jesus' early message had been summarized in the exhortation to repent of one's sin and to believe the good news that the Kingdom was at hand. The early Christians understood the resurrection of Christ as the establishment of the Kingdom of God, not as a final consummation—that act would come only at the end of history when Christ would return to judge the world—but as the established framework in which all of history would now move, and against which all historical events must now be evaluated.

Because both Jesus and the disciples believed that the Kingdom of God would come in a very short time, the teaching of Jesus and the work of the disciples centered around what the Kingdom would be like and what one must do to be ready for its final consummation in history.[1] To participate in the body of Christ was to participate in the reality of the Kingdom. Those who asked to be baptized had heard the Word and confessed their faith, but the New Testament makes it clear that faithfulness is more than belief, more than willingness to say "Jesus is Lord." The early Christians believed that Christ calls those who are doers of the Word and not hearers only.[2]

But what about those who do the work of Christ—deeds of justice, and love, and mercy—but who are not baptized into the community and do not confess that Christ is Lord? Are they participants in the Kingdom? This question has troubled Christian thought since the beginning.

On the one hand, Christians have generally been agreed that if Jesus is truly the Christ, then salvation means participation in the Kingdom which his body, the new community, symbolizes. To claim less than this would be to make no distinctive claim at all. The Roman Catholic church has put this matter most bluntly with the doctrine that there is no salvation outside the church.

On the other hand, Christian reflection has never been willing to identify the saved simply with those who have outwardly joined themselves with the Christian community, or even with a smaller group within the church who could be identified as doers of the Word, and not hearers only. Roman Catholic doctrine has often spoken of a "latent church," the unidentified community of those whose will and work was identified with Christ's will and work in the world, even when lacking outward, conscious acknowledgment of that loyalty.[3] Karl Rahner has recently spoken of this group as "anonymous Christians."[4] He has been criticized for a subtle form of the old Christian imperialism, but the point here is that the doctrine of the Kingdom in the history of Christian thought has regularly allowed for a measure of inclusiveness outside the official Christian community. The Kingdom has usually not been just for Christians.

This recognition that there are unidentified children of the Kingdom in the world outside Christianity expresses the conviction that God has nowhere been without witnesses. Within the Bible itself there are numerous occasions in which God's prophets point to those outside the community of believers as being the true servants of God in the world. This is characteristic of God's judgment on Israel. These prophetic proclamations are in keeping with the biblical conviction that

God is transcendent Lord of all history and that God's will works without restriction to those called to be "the people of God."

The most dramatic occasion of this kind in the Old Testament is the prophet Isaiah's proclamation concerning Cyrus of Persia. Isaiah's is not only the first biblical statement that gives a summary overview of how God acts in history; it is human culture's first statement of a theology of history. Combined with the later views of Saint Paul it becomes normative for Christian thought. For this reason, it is especially important to note that the central figure in Isaiah's proclamation—the one whom God has chosen to work his will in the world—is Cyrus of Persia, who was not a Jew, or even a seeker after Yahweh.[5]

The Israelites had become subject to the king of Babylon, and when they tried to rebel, the Babylonian armies were sent to crush the religion and carry off a group of the rebellious people into exile. Cyrus later defeated Babylon, thus freeing the Israelites to return home. For this community in exile, deliverance from the Babylonian captivity was and could only be an act of God's mercy and grace. By the same logic, the one through whom this deliverance came could be none other than a servant of God, because he was doing God's will. Thus Isaiah refers to Cyrus as the anointed one of the most high God. It is significant that, unlike other ancient texts that record the conquests of Cyrus, no mention is made in Isaiah of any inherent moral quality in the man or any particular righteousness in his motivation for fighting the Babylonians. The point is simply that he is doing what God wants done, even though he knows nothing of the Israelites' God and has no conscious intention of doing anything except achieving another conquest.

The Old Testament community was both more and less constricted in its self-understanding than the New Testament community. The Old Testament community was more constricted in the latent tribalism represented by the requirement of circumcision; but it was also less constricted in that it did

not worry about the abstract problem of whether other nations also pleased God. The answer seemed to them to lie in
the events of history, and the historical Cyrus had actually
been a servant of the Most High because he had done what
God wanted done. For Israel the only compelling issue was
to discover the will of God and do it.

The significance of Cyrus for the theology of Isaiah implies
that this same awareness of God's acting in history apart
from the community of his chosen ones was part of the self-
consciousness of the New Testament community. What was
the teaching of Jesus on this issue?

The idea of the Kingdom of God is central to Jesus' teaching and to his self-understanding of his mission. It has roots
in the Old Testament, even though that exact phrase is not
used. The Jewish Talmud speaks of "the coming age" and
also, perhaps most significantly, of "life." The Kingdom is the
realm of life which stands over against the life-denying powers
of sin and death.[6] There were three major aspects to ideas of
the Kingdom current in Jesus' time: (1) it was an eternal fact
of God's lordship over history; (2) it could be seen as a present
manifestation in the lives of men and women, for those able
to discern the signs of the times; and (3) it was a consummation still to come in the future, in a time that God would
choose.

The most characteristic form of Jesus' teaching was the
parable, and there are eleven recorded parables which begin
with some such phrase as "the Kingdom of heaven is like . . . "
Jesus' teaching about the Kingdom was radical, but there are
a number of popular misconceptions about what was distinctive in his view of the Kingdom. Among these is the often
quoted passage from Luke 17:21 sometimes translated "the
Kingdom of God is within you," thus making the Kingdom
a spiritual perception of individual inwardness akin to the
Neoplatonic views of Origen, the Vedantic views of Sankara,
and the contemporary views of psychologically oriented spirituality. The more accurate translation of the phrase, however—as in the contemporary Revised Standard Version of

the New Testament—is "the Kingdom of God is in the midst of you"; that is, in the community, not within an individual person. It is a social concept, not a personal one.

What was radical about Jesus' teaching was his emphasis on three new ideas about the Kingdom. First of all, he promised entrance to the Kingdom to the poor and the outcast, to tax collectors and sinners, and to those who were not Jews. Second, he presented his own ministry as a preliminary realization of the sovereignty of God in history. Third, he took the hope of the Kingdom with new seriousness and related it to the ethical life of the community, so that ethical action was given a new basis. Having already discussed the second of these three points, we need to reflect on the relation between the first and the third.

Jesus announced that the tax collectors and sinners would enter the Kingdom before the Pharisees, because the self-righteousness of the Pharisees prevented their repentance and humility. The Kingdom, Jesus said, was not for those with great learning like the scribes, but for those who could trust God and respond like little children. Most radically, however, he said that the Kingdom might well not be inherited by those sons of the Kingdom (Israel) but would be inherited instead by those who came from East and West and North and South, and who would sit at the table with Abraham, Isaac, and Jacob.

The context for this comment in Matthew 8:11–12 is a request from a Roman centurion who had asked Jesus to heal his servant who was lying paralyzed at home and in great distress. Jesus says that he will come and heal him. The centurion, however, says that Jesus need only "say the word, and my servant will be healed." Jesus marvels at the man's faith, and then comments that there will be many people like this man in the Kingdom. This theme is repeated elsewhere in the New Testament. Entrance into the Kingdom requires faith, the kind of trust and openness to God found in the responsiveness of children and the unquestioning confidence of the centurion.

The second requirement for entrance into the Kingdom which Jesus stresses in his parables is willingness to do the will of God. He warns that there will be many who say, "Lord, Lord," but who will not enter the Kingdom, even though they may have done mighty works in his name. Here he is criticizing those religionists who have made much of ceremonial observance but have not cared for those in human need.

The Kingdom is for those who have faith. The notion of faith in Matthew 25 means trust, openness, and confidence in one's neighbors and one's world. It is trust in and loyalty toward a God who rules over, cares for, and is present to all. This attitude is a fundamentally human experience of God. But Jesus also means faith as trust in his own power to do what is asked of him. The centurion sensed in Jesus the power to heal, and he trusted it.

When Jesus marvels at the faith of people in these situations, however, he is not marveling that they have understood him to be the Christ. He is marveling at the depth of their faith in God, as evidenced in their trust of him. The centurion is to sit at table in the Kingdom with Abraham, Isaac, and Jacob not because he recognized Jesus to be the Christ, but because he trusted Jesus to heal his servant. In this sense the Christ of the Gospels is unbound from the doctrinal formulations of Christian theology. There is no evidence that Jesus wanted these people of faith to join his group of followers. Even so, they are part of the Kingdom, because of their faith.

The parable of the last judgment makes the point that others will be part of the Kingdom, not because of their faith but because of their active love for their neighbors. The response to poverty, hunger, illness, and imprisonment is once again related to the presence of Jesus. In caring for the afflicted, these folk have cared for the Christ, even though they never affirmed trust in him or belief that he was the Christ. They have fulfilled the commandment to love the neighbor, and in so doing have served the Lord's Christ, without know-

ing the ultimate meaning of what they were doing. This idea
in Matthew's parable of the last judgment hints at the theme
of John's gospel: that Jesus is the Word of God through whom
all things are made. Relationship to him is therefore relationship not only to ourselves and to God who made us, but to
the neighbor whom God also made.[7]

As faith is trust in the goodness of one's world which
recognizes in Jesus a unique power to effect that goodness,
so love is the event of relationship to the neighbor which
participates in God's will for the world. Neither faith nor love
is an exclusively religious occasion. In this sense one cannot
speak of Muslim love, or Hindu love, or Christian love. Love
itself is simply itself. Because all people are beloved of God,
love is essentially a human possibility. Jesus recognizes this
in the parable of the last judgment, when humankind will be
judged on the basis of those occasions when they participated
in self-forgetting love for a neighbor. Because love is the living
basis of all religious ethics, in spite of different interpretations
of duty and ethical responsibility, Jesus' teachings and his
embodiment of those teachings are part of a universal human
religious heritage that is not limited to Christianity.[8]

The New Testament, for all its distinction between those
who are baptized into the church and those who are not,
recognizes that the new community in Christ is essentially the
new humanity of those whose loving faith makes them one
with God and their neighbors. Jesus, as the Christ, embodies
the Kingdom. He is the word of God, from the beginning,
because his life and death and resurrection are a definitive
story of God's love for humankind. To love God and the
neighbor is to participate in Christ's presence in the world,
even without naming the name, or recognizing that care for
the oppressed is care for Christ himself.

The New Testament idea of community is not limited to
what we know today as the Christian church. The fundamental community of New Testament thought is the Kingdom
of God, which is inaugurated historically in the new humanity

in Christ. The true body of the resurrected Lord is that community of faith and love which exists not only within the band of those who are baptized, but also in that larger company of the centurion who trusted Jesus to heal his servant, and those nameless lovers of humankind who selflessly care and are therefore counted among the blessed.

3

The Christian Problem

THE New Testament expectation of an imminent end to world history and an ushering in of the Kingdom of God became an embarrassment to subsequent Christian philosophies of history. Christians proclaimed Christ's resurrection as the sign that history was about to end, but when this did not happen, the meaning of the Christian view of history was no longer clear. Precisely what was being claimed? What did it mean to say that the Kingdom of God is the ultimate meaning of history and has been established in history, when the world historical process continues as before? What real difference had the resurrection of Jesus Christ made to the world historical process?

On a superficial level the question could be answered simply: the resurrection had produced the Christian church, which became an increasingly significant institution in Western history. But the Christian church did not add to the meaning of history for those who are not Christians, whereas the Christian message announced a radical transformation of history itself that affected everyone. The intellectual challenge for Christian thought was to show how the truth of the resurrection could have meaning even for those who might not believe it. This task was important in defending the faith from the criticisms of philosophers and other opinion makers in the Roman world. It was also important for defending the faith from heretics such as the Gnostics, who claimed to have the true interpretation of Jesus' life and death and resurrection. Finally, it was important for the task of Christian evangelism in a world familiar with philosophical argument.

No one would join the new community in Christ unless they understood the meaning of the Christian claim. And without the possibility of universal appeal Christianity would be denying its identity as the beginning of a new human community. Greek philosophy therefore became crucial for implementing the Christian mission, because it was no longer enough simply to tell the story about Jesus' life and death and resurrection, interpreting it in the theological categories of classical Jewish thought and experience as Paul had done. A universal message needed a universal coin of communication, and that was what philosophy provided.

The most influential of the early Christian philosophers was Augustine of Hippo.[1] As a young man he had endorsed, one after another, the major philosophical schools of his day, and he remained under the strong influence of Plato and Neoplatonism until the end of his life. This background stood him in good stead after his conversion to Christianity, since it gave him an insider's understanding of current philosophical views. More than any other single thinker, with the possible exception of Philo, he provided the terms in which Christian faith was to understand itself in its continuing struggle with Western secular culture.

Augustine was convinced that the Christian faith was not only the revelation of God's reality in himself, but also the meaning of human history. In order to save this view from intellectual obscurantism it was necessary for him to articulate those ideas and values that were distinctively Christian contributions to understanding the world historical process, and thus signs or marks of the Kingdom in history. He established the intellectual framework of two such categories. One is a Christian notion of selfhood; the other is a Christian interpretation of history. Augustine is the author of the first fully articulated philosophy of history, the *City of God*.[2] He is also the author of the first major autobiography in the Western intellectual tradition, the *Confessions*.[3]

Augustine's doctrine of the essence of the individual, the soul, was distinctive in relating the soul to that element of selfhood which combines bodily desire with intellectual and spiritual awareness: the will. This doctrine preserved the biblical perspective of Matthew's parable of the Kingdom and its insistence that love for God becomes real when it is translated into moral action. In the dividedness of the human will Augustine discovered the key to the human situation. As Paul had argued before him, the critical problem of human inwardness is not that our pure spirits are bound by a base world of things, but that our will is morally at war with itself: "I do not do the good I want, but the evil I do not want is what I do."[4] For Augustine, the human soul incorporates the goodness of humankind, derived from our archetypal memory that we are made in the image of God, and it yearns to be with him. At the same time, because we are human and not God, the soul also incorporates the desire to live in the world for the fulfillment of our own desires apart from God. Sin, as our estrangement from God, is both a condition of our humanity and the temptation of our wills to which we regularly succumb.

The will is the activity of the soul for Augustine. Its spiritual and moral ambivalence is the fundamental human problem. The critical issue for human life is therefore not some abstract knowing of an eternal truth, but a concrete activation of our wills in accordance with the will of God. Augustine's *Confessions* is his personal story of grappling with this issue. Salvation, for him, was tied to concrete issues of personal morality and vocational decision.

In this theology of will Augustine set the terms for the subsequent development of the notion of individual selfhood in the tradition of Western philosophy. Individuals do indeed participate in a transcendent reality of Spirit, which is of God.

The sources of human dignity are therefore within the individual human being. But that essential goodness of the human
individual is not a distorted appearance of a universal cosmic
goodness, nor is it to be fulfilled in a release from the realm
of the earthly and empirical. It is a characteristic of the living,
historic individual, here and now, which is activated in the
individual's relations with the world. Because the soul is expressed in the will, and because the will is active, the soul
becomes real in the individual's active response to the community. This is the meaning of Jesus' judgment in Matthew's
parable of the Kingdom.

The true essence of each individual person is not a secret,
ideal, inner meaning, discontinuous with life in the world.
Soul is the personal meaning of our individual relations with
others in the human community. Hence we are to be judged
by the character of those relationships. We are essentially
actors in history, not temporarily embodied divine essences.
Social institutions must therefore take account of our historical status as persons. This view of the self as person makes
possible the political development from subject to citizen in
modern Western forms of government. The Augustinian idea
of the self is fundamental to modern theories of human rights
and to the democratic philosophy of the state.

Augustine's *City of God* provided a major impetus in that
direction. The *Confessions* had marveled at the capacity of
the self to transcend itself through the seemingly limitless
range of memory. The restless heart reaches back in memory
to the almost forgotten sense of itself as fashioned in the image
of the Transcendent One. In spite of our recalcitrant wills,
salvation is possible for us all because, as in Plato's view that
knowing is remembering, the proclamation of God's Word
can jog the memory we all have of God as model and maker
of ourselves. We love him and yearn for him partly because
he is the meaning of our being ourselves.

But what of the future? Pure nostalgia for the lost good
of the soul's home leads to cynicism at worse, and Stoicism
at best. In either event, the experience of life in the world is

held at arm's length. It is suffered because we have no alternative. Whatever else can be said of our historic existence—
that it is good for us in disciplining our spirits, or a necessary evil to be endured—the backward look at transcendence produces no historic hope or glimmer of meaning in
history.

The *City of God* is Augustine's affirmation of friendship
with the future. Ever since the fall of Adam, he tells us, humankind has been afflicted by divided loyalties. One great city
has served God, finding the meaning of its own will in God's
will. The other city has rebelled against God, serving the devil
and those angels and demons who placed themselves over
against God.

Jerusalem and Babylon were the symbolic cities in Augustine's schema, with Cain and Abel as their historic pro-
genitors. The citizens of God's city are always pilgrims, in the
world but not of it; homesick, restless, uprooted, yearning for
a far country. This longing for God sets them off from those
whose true heart's desire is elsewhere.

A Christian philosophy of community is concerned with
humankind, universally. It is inevitably embodied in a philosophy of history, which sets forth principles for understanding this universal human story. The philosophy of history that
Augustine finally developed was distinct both from his earlier
view of prophetic history (shared by most of his Christian
contemporaries) and from the universal history of his secular
protagonists. Prophetic history was a sectarian account of
those events in which God had blessed his people, but it had
nothing at all to say about the history of the secular world.
In this view, the events in which God leads his chosen people
are a thread of light woven through a blanket of darkness.
Secular humankind is left to wander God-forsakenly through
the aimless doing and undoing of their ahistorical fate. For
Augustine, however, God's goodness was evident in non-
Christian events as well: in the brilliant arguments of pagan
philosophers, and even in the heroic loyalty of rogues and
thieves to one another. Although his early writings followed

this prophetic history, it was too small a vehicle for his vision in the *City of God*.

The universal history of the Neoplatonists, on the other hand, had great scope, but that was its problem. Porphyry had hold of the meaning of the entire historical process, but he understood particular historic events as universal demonstrations of immutable principles. For Porphyry, therefore, the historic process is a symbol; the reality of history is what it means. For Augustine, this transcendental intellectualism failed to explain why actual events are as they are, but he was challenged by Porphyry to make Christianity relevant to the sweep of the centuries. In so doing, Augustine argued that Christianity is not simply one religion among the world's many, but the natural religion of humankind. This radical claim required a philosophy of history that could show how Christian faith solved the common human problem.

That problem, as Augustine understood it, resulted from a tension between the two cities, based on the conflict between Cain and Abel. Cain, who hoped for no more than he could see, founded the first city for those who are firmly at home and rooted in the world. Augustine believed that the most deeply felt human need is for peace, both within oneself and in one's interrelationships with others.

In the city of Cain, peace is found in balance, order, and control of our inner appetites and the outward conflict of wills in society. But the settled folk of this *civitas mundi* envy those who have a vision beyond worldly accommodation to social engineering. They are pilgrims yearning for a greater good, living in the spirit rather than through law. It was envy that caused Cain to slay Abel, and it is envy that creates the antagonism between the city of man and the city of God throughout human history.

In his earlier *Contra Faustum*, Augustine used the Cain and Abel conflict as an allegory, a dramatic pattern prefiguring and illuminating the central story of Christ's death. In the *City of God*, however, the Cain and Abel story is an archetype as understood by classical Greek dramatists and contemporary Jungian psychoanalysis. It is a pattern of fundamental human behavior; it is not a theoretical interpretation of an abstraction called human nature, but a concrete principle that actually explains why people do what they do. Christianity, therefore, is not a religion for an empire, like Rome, or a cultural community, like Israel. It is the natural religion of humankind; it is the meaning of being human.[5]

In making this argument, however, Augustine was careful to distinguish his position from that of the Neoplatonists, especially Plotinus. The Augustinian pilgrim is much like the authentic philosopher of Plotinus, who also yearns for a distant country; but, unlike the Neoplatonists and the Advaitins of the Hindu tradition, Augustine's vision is not centered on a flight of the alone to the Alone. The place he yearns for is a heavenly city, the Kingdom of God, but the common cake of custom in any particular historical situation contains a foretaste of that Kingdom, found in those goods of ordinary life which God gives us in plenty. Christian faith is therefore not the key to a truth that lies outside our historic existence; it is the concrete meaning of what human experience is for us all. It is what life is all about.

Augustine's view needs to be understood against the background of his purpose in writing *City of God*. Initially he set out to answer critics of Christianity who argued that the sack of Rome had been made possible by the spread of Christian faith and the subsequent decline of Roman religion. Rome's gods had inspired civic virtue, and Christianity, it was argued, now sapped political morals and morale in substituting its vision of a universal human community for the local loyalty to Rome. In the process of making his case, however, Augustine became increasingly persuaded that the real issue was not whether civil society was being corrupted by Christianity, but whether Christianity was being corrupted by civil society.

His elaborate defense of God's inscrutability in regard to history is, in part, protection against co-opting Christianity as a civil religion. He was protecting the universality of the

Christian community from the tribalism of Roman religion. This was important because Christianity was not a private religion. It understood itself as functioning within society in many of the same ways that had been characteristic of pagan religion.

This was a new situation. For Jesus and the immediate post-resurrection Christian community, the coming of the Kingdom was so imminent that the problem of Christ's long-range relation to culture did not arise. Now, however, the question for Christians was the relation between their tight bond with one another in the church and their loose bond with others in the larger secular community. How is it possible to be "in the world" but not "of the world"? How is it possible to be a loyal citizen of the state, and still loyal to the God who transcends and rules over all states? And if, with Augustine, one sees God's power and presence in both the church and the world, how is one to understand God's saving work of preparing this world for the coming of the Kingdom?

The New Testament view is that the Spirit comes upon individuals and makes of them a body that is the continuing body of Christ. This body is the new community in Christ and is the beginning of a new humanity. Because Christ establishes the Kingdom of God in history, this new community in Christ *is* the Kingdom of God. To say that history continues, however, is to say that the Kingdom is established as promise, not fulfillment; that the sin of humankind still struggles against the grace of God; that the present age of history is a period between the times of the cross and the coming of the Kingdom in power.

To say that God is at work in our present history to fulfill the promise of the Kingdom is not to say that this fulfillment will come entirely from within the historical process. The power that finally fulfills the promise of the Kingdom, according to the biblical stories of the end of history, will come from outside the historical process itself when Christ returns in glory to judge the quick and the dead.

On the other hand, the present age is not a time of passive waiting or of simply holding at bay the forces of human sin. In doing God's will in the world the pilgrim people of God are helping to prepare the times for the coming of the Kingdom in power. God acts through the new humanity in Christ to reveal the nature of the kingdom and to prepare history for its rightful ruler.

To ask what it means to say that God works in history is not primarily to solve a theological conundrum; it is to seek the foundation of Christian morale. In a world where goodness is regularly defeated, only the heroically strong or curiously mindless will be able to keep on serving the good for the simple sake of keeping on. The rest of us need to know that what we are doing at least counts for something in the economy of God and is making a difference in the historical process. It is not enough, therefore, to know that individual acts of sacrificial love are cherished in the heart of God if they are only occasional gleams in the dark night of history.

On the other hand, it would be too awfully grand of us to regard ourselves as actually bringing in the Kingdom. If our morale needs some good hope that our labor is not in vain, it also needs some humbling assurance that the venture is not totally dependent on the steadfastness of our labor. Given the fact of human sin, the Kingdom will have to be given by God, not made by humankind. Our freedom to struggle and fail and struggle again rests on the good hope that God is working his purpose out, whether through us or in spite of us.

Christian living centers on trust in God, not in achieving virtue. To trust God is to respond to God's call; to be judged, chastened, and punished for the failures of that response; and to be called and respond again because God's judgment is always merciful, and God's continual judging and redeeming presence is the only sure healing for the hurt which is our humanity.

In rejecting the prophetic history of Christian sectarianism, and in making philosophy a legitimate form of Christian reflection, Augustine opens the Christian community to the realization that the world and its ways of thinking are not radically alien. It is, after all, God's world, and God is at work in its worldliness to promote the purposes of the Kingdom. Christians now have a responsibility to the state and to the culture. No longer is it possible to deal with problems of citizenship glibly by suggesting that one render to Caesar the things that are Caesar's, and to God the things that are God's. No longer is it possible to deal with problems of culture scornfully by suggesting that philosophy is, in Paul's unhappy phrase, "vain deceit."

Christianity's contribution to the Western culture which, for a time, bore its name, was extensive, as historians like Toynbee and philosophers like Whitehead have made clear. Our question, however, is what contribution Christian life and thought made to the larger notion that we are all part of a universal human community. If there is to be a world civilization, what common loyalty will hold us all together?[6] The early Christian community struggled mightily over a rather modest challenge to its ethnic homogeneity. Once it opened itself to the Hellenistic world, the idea of "all sorts and conditions" of people took on radical new meaning. Most crucial was the seed of individualism that had been sown in the notion that each person was to be honored in his or her own right as a child of God, regardless of whether that person were Jew or Greek, slave or free, male or female. In the modern world this idea became so dominant that it virtually defined modern culture.

The original Christian notion of community, of course, had been fashioned in a traditional culture where natural bonds determined one's fellows. In place of these natural bonds, the Christian community substituted a transcendent bond of love and loyalty to a God who included all. That worked effectively as long as the culture was determined by Christian faith. For the early church, as a small sect anticipating the early end of the world, Christianity was its culture. And before the early church had completely absorbed the fact that the world was not about to end, Constantine made Christianity the official religion of an empire that spanned the known world. So, in very different terms, Christianity and culture continued their bond.

With theology as queen of the sciences in medieval culture, all was well. But when the modern era introduced individualism as a secular value in its own right, Christian life and thought were faced with a new challenge. Modern Western history was developing the notion that the individual human being is to be valued and accorded certain fundamental human rights, not by virtue of anything that he or she does, but by virtue of who he or she is.[7]

This is not a natural given, like the givenness of one's situation in a traditional society. It was, rather, a way of transforming the great gift of a traditional society—the absolute assurance of one's identity and one's sense of being at home—into a viable, modern form. Here the bond is creedal, or ideological, rather than natural. It depends not on where you were born, or family bloodlines, class position, language, or religion, but on an individual decision to be part of this community of loyalty to this common cause. Some, at least, with "eyes of faith," discerned the hand of God in this development.[8]

The American experiment in nation building was the culmination of Western modernity's engagement with this new idea. We need to have a close look at what the American experiment was all about. Before we do that, however, we need some sense of the pervasiveness of the idea of the individual as it affected not only modern Western science and philosophy but modern Western social and political thought as well.

Part II

4

Modern Homelessness and the Individual

THE best fruit of modern individualism was the new freedom of choice which increasingly gave individuals control over their own lives. The price paid for it, however, was a sense of homelessness and loneliness in the modern mind and spirit. Hegel notes that the possibility of being culturally "lost" arose first in the Roman world where the spread of empire had created a cultural maelstrom. Traditional cultures had been thrown together in the same political structure without any natural, instinctive, or inherent bonding among them. The empire was held together by the efficiency of Roman administration and the power of the Roman army, not by any felt sense among people in North Africa and Asia Minor that they were now identified with, and committed to, that faraway abstraction called Rome.

In the modern world, this sense of lostness has become acute because we face the cultural maelstrom alone as individuals, not as members of a family or tribe.[1] Homelessness is the spiritual price paid for modernity's great adventure in reshaping its world. It is not the result of an external force being exercised upon us against our will, such as Roman power. It is something we have done to ourselves, in the process of gaining what Francis Bacon called "the greatest jewel." That jewel was a method in the natural sciences that made it possible not only to understand nature, but also to control it and make it work for human purposes. The importance of these developments in modern science was that they made permanent cultural changes in the West which, in turn, put the problem of community in a new light.

In a traditional society, the individual's relation to the three fundamental elements of experience—oneself, other selves, and nature—is given. That is what tradition means. One is an instinctive participant in one's own life, in the social life of the community, and in the larger order of nature in a manner given by tradition and understood by common consensus. Modern individualism, however, achieves its social, political, and scientific goals by analyzing those connections and thus breaking them down. The breakdown is necessary for an empirical science if it is to understand the behavior patterns of individual elements in the natural world, in isolation from other individual elements. Empiricism requires an initial disconnection of individuals from one another. The breakdown is also necessary in society and politics if the individual person is to be free. The price paid for this freedom, however, is the loss of connection, of tradition's sense of being at home in the world—at home with oneself, with one's neighbors, and with one's natural surroundings.

The pervasiveness of personal loneliness in the modern world will be more comprehensible after a brief reflection on the way modern philosophy has led to metaphysical loneliness, especially in the alienation of ourselves from nature and from society.

The medieval interpreters of Aristotle integrated the human philosophical *eros* for understanding the "reasons why" (*to dioti*) things are as they are with the divine *agape*, which is God's will that things should be so. In that context, science was human wisdom conjoined with divine truth. In the Elizabethan period, however, there was a major shift in the understanding of science, popularized by Francis Bacon in his insistence that the aim of science is useful knowledge. On this view, knowledge becomes power *over* the forces of physical nature. No longer is science concerned with pure knowing for its own sake. Science is now increasingly concerned with what Americans call "know how," or ways to exercise physical control over natural process. As Bacon put it so eloquently, "I will give thee the greatest jewel I have. For I will impart to thee, for the love of God and men, a relation of the true state of Salomon's House. . . . The end of our foundation is the knowledge of causes and secret motions of things, and the enlarging of the bounds of human empire, to effecting of all things possible."[2]

For the Greeks, science had been elegant explanation, a fit pursuit for lofty minds to whom affluence had granted leisure to reflect on principles of understanding. For medieval Christianity, science had been the faithful uncovering of the ways in which God effected his will in the world. But for Bacon and his successors, science explored the laws of matter in motion, and nature was to be obeyed in order to be commanded. The purpose of scientific study was "to turn heaven and earth to the use and welfare of mankind." Power and possession thus became the keynote of modern thought.

In principle there was no limitation to the new possibility for science. The principles of power and control were open-ended and indiscriminate in serving human ambitions; they were without reference to Christian wisdom as service for God, or Greek wisdom as service for the good life. The morality of the new science was the obligation to explore all things possible, without hindering the open quest for truth through the limiting notions of faithfulness to God or conformity to some universal Good.

The harsh manipulation of nature that often resulted was given moral sanction by a view that relieved nature of quality and purpose. This was in sharp contrast to the medieval view of science inherited from Aristotle. For Aristotle, a theory of knowledge was precisely a theory of the world's intelligibility, in which the power of the knower to know a thing joined with the power of the thing to be known.

Notable here is Aristotle's understanding of a physical object. In order to understand any particular thing one needs to know the forces or causes that have made it what it is. For Aristotle, there were four of these. The material cause is the stuff out of which the thing is made. A maple tree is made of wood, for example. Then there is the efficient cause, which sets in motion the generation of the thing, in this case the seed falling into suitable soil. The third cause is the formal cause, or the particular kind which determines this particular thing. The reason that maple seeds grow into maple trees rather than oaks is that they are a maple kind of seed, and this kind is the formal cause. Fourth, there is the final cause, which is Aristotle's name for the purpose of a thing. The purpose of the tree is to be a real, or perfected, maple. In its career from seed to sapling the maple tree is aiming at something. Just as a growing boy is aiming at manhood, so a growing sapling is aiming at becoming a full-grown tree.

This notion that the natural world has purpose of some sort is part of Aristotle's view of the world as intelligible, and intelligibility is not radically different for natural things than it is for persons. Natural objects participate in the knowing process. For Aristotle a yellow wall has the power to be seen as yellow. So knowing something is not solely the function of an individual mind. It is a natural function within an intelligible world in which both the power of the individual knower to know and the power of the thing to be known participate.

In contrast, modern epistemologies from Bacon and Descartes to Kant are primarily interested in knowledge as the power of the individual mind to know. Descartes, initiating the modern view that physical objects are to be understood in terms of the laws of matter in motion, understood nature primarily in terms of material and efficient causes. The formal cause is not inherent in the thing itself, but rather in the way we understand and talk about what kind of thing it is. The formal cause is a function of signs and symbols of understanding in the mind, rather than the inherent intelligibility of the thing itself. And the final cause is removed from metaphysical analysis altogether. We no longer speak of a tree as having any natural purpose.

In his famous meditation on a piece of beeswax, Descartes noted that the shape, color, texture, and even smell of the wax was changed radically when it was heated and melted.[3] Its primary quality—the one feature that remained constant throughout conceivable changes in its outward form—was that it continued to take up space. Hence Descartes's definition of physical objects as *res extensa* ("extended things"), objects that were locatable in space. The mind, on the other hand, was obviously radically different in kind since it was not locatable in space. Mind, said Descartes, is *res cogitans* (a "thinking thing"). Hence the modern notion of an object or thing. "Things" do not have inherent purposes of their own, as minds do. Things are matter, and minds have no moral obligation toward matter. Here is the epistemological root of our contemporary ecological crisis, where the spirit of Bacon's notion that science seeks "the effecting of all things possible" joins with the Cartesian notion that "things" do not participate in the scientific process of knowing, and hence can lay no moral claim on the knower or the knower's purposes.

Descartes's reflection on the piece of beeswax lays the groundwork for the modern problem of knowledge. Building on the Augustinian view that all knowledge is grounded in the absolutely certain and immediate knowledge that one has of one's own mind, Descartes admits that our knowledge of physical nature and our knowledge of minds other than our own becomes problematic. The structure of the problem becomes clear as he reflects engagingly on the metaphysical status of the particular piece of wax he holds in his hand. Does the same wax remain after this change? We can all agree that it does. Previously, however, we thought we knew this particular piece of stuff to be beeswax by its shape, color, feel, taste, and smell; that is to say, by our sense perception of it. Now it is clear that the wax, in its essential waxness, remains even when all of these qualities we sensed in it are gone.

So for all the fact that science must begin its exploration with sense perception of particular objects, our true knowledge of any particular is not rooted in sense perception. Sense perceptions change while the essential thing remains. Real perception is essentially an intuition of the mind.

With this feathery touch of brilliance, Descartes initiated a seismic shift in the foundations of the modern mind. Aristotle's natural realism celebrates a sunny and untroubled confidence that the world is a coherent whole in which my mind, other minds, and physical nature are integrated by a *Nous* (world mind) which, while primarily evident in the workings of your mind and mine, is also evident in the structure and functional operations of physical nature. Hence the entire experienced world is illumined with the light of intelligibility. In such a world human minds are not radically separated from nature, nor is my mind fundamentally at a loss to explain its instinctive assurance that you, who are distinct from me, also have a mind of your own.

With the Cartesian shift, however, illumination no longer floods the world. The light of reason illuminates the inwardness of the individual mind. *Cogito, ergo sum.* The mind of my neighbor, however, although not quite covered with darkness is, to me, a twilight of confusion. We all know perfectly well that the neighbor has a mind precisely like our own, but our "other minds problem" expresses our inability to explain to ourselves how we know this.

The natural world, on the other hand, is not in twilight; it is cast into an epistemological outer darkness. To define a physical object as *res extensa* is to announce a mystery. We know that there is something out there, and we know how it appears to us, but we cannot know what it is in itself. Aristotle knew the "treeness" of the tree from the inside, because he knew its purpose in being that kind of tree. The implications of the Cartesian view were later made specific by Kant, when he pointed out that all knowing begins with the reality of the individual knower. He observes, irrefutably, that I can know only what I know. All that I know is logically preceded by the realization that I am knowing it. This "I think" must be presupposed in any knowledge claim by any mind.[4] Any particular act of knowing is thus radically relativized. What the object may be in and for itself must always be unknown to me.

For the modern mind, knowledge of nature thus became knowledge from the "outside." The individualization of the knowing process aggrandized the power of the individual mind as the sole active agent in the knowing process. Perception is now, to use T. S. Eliot's phrase, a raid on the unknowable, a bequeathing of status and reality on that which, apart from the mind's gracious attention, must remain dark and dumb. Aristotle's nature, enlivened by the purposive presence of the world *Nous*, here becomes shrouded and alien.

Aristotle's world was a metaphysical community. Its lines of connection made intelligible the relations among individuals, their fellows, and the natural world that was their setting. In breaking down our understanding of these relations, modernity has sacrificed that visceral sense of community which lets us feel at home in our experienced world of ourselves, others, and nature.

Without some understanding of these relations, religious faith becomes obscurantist. What would it mean to believe in God without understanding one's relation to God in the world of nature and society which God creates? With no clear answer to this question the spiritual life of individuals becomes increasingly isolated. Solipsism, the metaphysics of loneliness, becomes the hidden order of the day in philosophy. As a result, fear inevitably becomes a major consideration in social and political thought. And the nostalgia for a genuine community becomes the inarticulate passion of an entire culture.[5]

The predominance of the individual mind in the knowing process is fundamental to the role individuality plays in various expressions of modern thought, from the emphasis on induction in scientific empiricism to the later rise of romanticism, existentialism, and depth psychology, where individual experience determines reality. Most significant for our purposes, however, is the effect of modern individuality on theories of the state. Thomas Hobbes's *Leviathan* is the first major indication of this fundamental change, since he is the first modern philosopher to apply the principles of the new science to social philosophy.

With his roots in the medieval Ockhamite philosophy, which held that only individual things are real, Hobbes explored the social implications of the new physics. A thoroughgoing mechanist, he was profoundly impressed by Galileo's view of a universe that was, as Hobbes liked to say, "nothing but" bodies in motion. Hobbes's vision of the world is cause-tight and logically necessary; for him causality is "nothing but" the efficient force of motion on body, whether one is exploring the heavens above or the inward nature of the human soul.

For Descartes, the external world of *res extensa* was not intelligible in itself, but our perception of it was intelligible because perception, for him, was an intuition of the mind. And for Spinoza, cause as known to the mind was always a formal notion, thus inherently intelligible as an idea. But for Hobbes, even thought is to be explained as a mechanical contact between bodies. Knowledge itself is a "motion in the internal substance of the head."[6]

By reducing thought itself to the brute fact of mechanical interaction, which is inherently unintelligible, Hobbes poses a paradox that has haunted subsequent generations of empiricists: a mechanical philosophy seeks to explain a world which, in its own terms, is inherently inexplicable. Hobbes was fascinated with the power of mathematical physics to provide a commonsense explanation of experience in its crude immediacy. By cutting the tie between explanation and intelligibility, however, Hobbes inadvertently fathered a school of philosophy that had no tools for understanding a metaphysics of ultimate meaning.

Because there is no logical relation among bodies in Hobbes's view, but only random action and reaction, there can be no natural bonds in human society, but only the continual conflict of individual wills over what I desire as opposed to what you desire. Hobbes inherited from Augustine and Calvin the conviction that, above all else, humankind desires peace. The conviction was deepened by his experience of civil strife and was made poignant by his personal neurotic timidity. He argued that it is our fear of one another that is the true basis of the human commonwealth.

In the light of his fear, self-interest dictates a social contract that will protect us from "the natural lusts of men (which) do daily threaten each other," because "all men in the state of nature have a desire and will to hurt."[7] As with natural science, so now with the science of government: the critical issue is power and control over a billiard-ball world of individual bodies in motion, so that they will not continually bump into each other.

Aristotle's nature embodied the purposive movement of life, for which the dynamics of human intelligibility were normative. With Hobbes the norm is the new mechanistic physics, and human life is interpreted not as a coherent thrust to fulfill its own purpose in being, but as incoherent clashes of alien bodies in continuous conflict. His solution is a social contract in which individuals give up some rights to a free exercise of will in exchange for protection by an all-powerful sovereign, who alone can provide coherence and safety in the commonwealth.

Hobbes's social theory continues to be influential because of its realism. He took seriously the extent of human selfishness. Those advocates of world community who hold to the fond dream that we can all learn to love one another, and thereby live in peace, need to reread their Hobbes. And, while Hobbes is no democrat, he firmly establishes an increasingly influential modern approach to social theory. Social philosophy must begin with the individual citizen in understanding the state, as though—for all our selfishness and sin—individuals are more and more the focal point of inherent dignity and worth. But with Hobbes there can be no question of

community, since there is no bonding notion of intelligibility
in the world as he conceives it, nor are there elements in human
psychology that tie us to our fellows.

Leviathan initiates a notion of society in which fear forges
the necessary social instruments for human cooperation. "Society" has no fundamental status in the nature of things
because it is always an artificial construct. For Hobbes community is not natural, or given, or fundamental in human
affairs. He has a well worked-out doctrine of the individual,
and he has reflected shrewdly and realistically on the possibilities for individuals cooperating in the construction of a
commonwealth. But that construction is always an artifice; it
does not, in his view, reflect a given structure of human community, such as that implied in the Christian understanding
of ourselves as creatures in God's creation.

The hierarchical world of medieval feudalism was a world
ordained by God and fraught with signs of divine power and
presence. But for medieval philosophy the notion of social
order was understood deductively from theological first principles. With Hobbes, modern science, working inductively,
produces social theory from below. It is empirical in intent.
It is not burdened with lofty first principles to which it must
be faithful. It is challenged by lowly facts which it must
explain.

Hobbes's social contract is not an event that takes place
in time, however; it is the continually self-renewing basis on
which alone human cooperation is possible. Here the seeds
of secularism are already being sown. For Hobbes, the Christian notion of community—the Kingdom of God—is no
longer a primary source for social theory. It is, rather, a still-
prestigious secondary reinforcement for a somewhat different
theory that has already been worked out inductively through
empirical observation and rational analysis. Christianity is,
indeed, the formal capstone of the Hobbesian commonwealth,
but this formal authority of God is only reinforcement for the
substantive laws of reason and the power of the sovereign.
The laws of God are therefore no longer primary operations

in relation to the commonly perceived laws of nature; they are only a distinctive way of speaking about those laws.

In a Christian culture, this way of speaking provides transcendental reinforcement to the way a people understand their world. But since this is now only an additional way of describing those laws that we know best and most surely as laws of nature, it is a way of speaking that is not necessary and eventually becomes only curious. It finally lapses altogether in a post-Christian culture. Christian claims to truth can command the interest of a secular culture only if they are integrated into the culture's understanding of itself. Hobbes related the two but didn't integrate them. Self, society, and nature are bound together only by principles of mechanics, which is to say that they are not genuinely bound together at all.

In Hobbes's world, Christian faith maintains a cultural position of honor and impotence—like a contemporary British monarch—fondly regarded but totally ignored when serious business is at hand. Had Hobbes taken his own neurotic fears more seriously as a philosophical problem he would have seen that he had not answered his own question. Locked doors give a measure of protection, but they do not quiet fear; and social contracts with those intent on "the will to hurt" provide precious little security.

A locked house is a prison, not a home; a contract state may make a workable social machine, but it is not a community. Fundamental to our age of anxiety is the yearning to feel at home in the world. An autonomous culture can rediscover relationships among the self, other selves, and nature only through some common ground of intelligibility and meaning that can integrate them.

The Great Wars of the twentieth century indicated the end of modernity's optimistic hope that technological control over physical nature could single-handedly create human well-being. The theoretical physics that made the atom bomb possible had already ushered in a new era of reflection on the nature of the physical universe.[8] The Newtonian notion of efficient causality, assuming that objects could be moved only by direct force—that causality is always local—had been superseded by quantum theory and its experimental discovery that electrons can be displaced without any local contact. Its reduction of physical nature to units of energy is one of several attacks on the Cartesian subject-object paradigm. Whitehead's process theory of "actual occasions" is another. It rejects the notion of matter as an ultimate metaphysical category. Husserl's phenomenology abandons the radical dualism of the Cartesian paradigm with a more holistic view of knowing as an idea-event, in which the essence of a phenomenon can be directly apprehended. William James's notion of "pure experience" as the metaphysical matrix out of which both subjectivity and objectivity are born is another expression of twentieth-century philosophy in search of a new metaphysical model of communal interrelationship among the three fundamental objects of human experience.

The rise of democracy, with its transformation of subjects into citizens, is clearly an expression of modern autonomy and has its beginnings in Hobbes's notion of *Leviathan*. For Hobbes, however, the exercise of individual choice precedes the formation and functioning of any actual state. The social contract is part of the myth of the state. The operation of *Leviathan* is in fact more medieval than modern, since functional power is delegated by the sovereign, not decided by the citizenry. The American experiment creates a new social myth: that all people are created equal; that they are endowed by their Creator with certain inalienable rights, chiefly the right to liberty; and that this liberty involves a continuing decisive role for individuals in the function of government.

American democracy is therefore a development of modernity's idealization of individuality and self-sufficiency. At the same time, however, America announces itself as a new kind of community. But how can one have a community based on the autonomous rights of free individuals? According to Hobbes's theory, the social contract dissolves at the point where the state fails to protect its citizenry; that is, in time of war. However, it is precisely at such times that national morale tends to be highest. Clearly the contract theory of the state has overlooked critical elements in community morale that are not "contracted" but are of considerable influence.

The myth of the state would seem to rely on elements of loyalty and love, as well as fear. Especially in the American experiment with individual human rights, democracy relies on an impulse toward community that is presupposed and remains unspecific in the course of national life. In order to withstand the conflicting pressures of individuals, each claiming his or her own individual rights, the sense of community must run deep enough to touch fundamental elements of trust and confidence in a particular people. This community-enabling element in the myth of democracy could be expected to parallel the individual-enabling element, the affirmation that all people are created equal.

This affirmation of equality is not a statement of fact. It is not an empirical description of how a democratic society deals with its citizenry. It is, rather, an element of national creed that becomes a principle of the national constitution, if not always effected in specific laws. The community-enabling element in the democratic myth is also part of the creed, but because it is religious in character, and because the conflict among formal religious institutions is a threat to individual rights, it will remain informal and generalized in the course of national life.

American democracy is a clear example of modernity's fascination with individuality and self-sufficiency, and, at the same time, it represents one of modernity's bravest ventures in community building.

5

Civil Religion and the American Dream

TRADITIONAL societies identify individuals in terms of their familial blood relations, their geographic region, language, class or caste, and religion. In all of these relations, individuality is secondary. One's personal rights, social status, and legal standing are derived from the primary reality of the natural/cultural groups with which one is identified. The group has solidarity and identity through the natural force of these traditional bonds.

The myth of the American dream, on the other hand, envisioned a melting pot in which the dross of tradition and its loyalties would be refined into a new loyalty to a national ideal. The *metanoia* of the melting pot would supposedly create an individual who, as American, was without regard for his or her racial, religious, or cultural background. Ideally, one's self-identifying cultural color would be blended into the bright, shining universalism of the American creed.[1] All Americans would be regarded as "endowed by their Creator with certain inalienable Rights." The essential selfhood of the new American would be derived not from the natural bonds of traditional culture but from a new belief in one's inherent right to individual freedom and its opportunities.

Liberty was America's watchword, and America's myth. In an unprecedented manner, America sought to extend this liberty to people of various backgrounds, thus giving substance to its ideology. Through free education for all its citizens, equal opportunity would supposedly exist for all. America's mythology has thrived on tales of immigrants who arrived penniless on its shores, soon to become millionaires by dint of hard work and native wit, and of young backwoods scholars, of flawless virtue and unflagging zeal, who read books by firelight and grew up to be president.

This lofty idea found some credibility in the hope for a new life in America's vast, unexplored, virgin land. The "virginity" of this "promised land" had both theoretical and practical consequences for the American dream. On the theoretical side it made possible the notion of space for a new beginning. In Puritan New England this notion was expressed theologically by analogy to "a city set upon a hill," a New Jerusalem, and even, in some Puritan preaching, to a new Eden where freedom of worship would be possible. In succeeding generations, as this theological ideal became generalized and secularized, the promise of religious freedom was expanded into constitutional guarantees for freedom of movement, freedom of the press, free speech, and freedom of political belief. At that point the American land became a symbolic land of opportunity where one was challenged to rise to whatever height one's innate capacities might take one.

On the practical side, the ideology of unlimited opportunity and the promise of wealth for the industrious was given substance by the availability of cheap farmland. All of America was theoretically promising, but if one found New York crowded and dirty, one could try an entirely different kind of life in rural Ohio. And if the granite boulders in New Hampshire's pastures made farming too backbreaking, there was rich bottom land in Illinois which, for a time, could be had for the asking.

Puritan New England initiated two fundamental motifs of the American dream. One was the trust that one's destiny was guided by a transcendent power, a conviction that undergirded American optimism and idealism. The other was Yankee ingenuity, the imaginative practicality that gave Americans their reputation for inventiveness and productivity. In spite of the prevailing opinion in Boston, however, the definitive event of American life was not what Van Wyck Brooks's too-gentle metaphor called "the flowering of New England."[2] New England burned with a zeal for the transcendent and exhibited remarkable physical and emotional toughness, but it was economically tight-fisted, religiously orthodox, and morally guilt-ridden. For all its gifts, New England knew nothing of spaciousness. Frederick Jackson Turner argues persuasively that the sense of space, openness, and opportunity that inspired the westward movement became crucial for the American dream.[3]

The spaciousness of the land also made possible the gradual adaptation of various ethnic groups into the American community. Immigrants with a common ethnic background could settle together, transposing their old culture and language for a period, gaining self-confidence and a sense of place before the ceaseless mobility of the New World eroded their traditionalism and gradually worked them into the mainstream of American life. Reinhold Niebuhr, to whom we shall soon turn, was such an immigrant.

The myth of the American dream was that this coequal American, stripped of race, creed, and religion, standing on individual rights, was now free to take advantage of virtually unlimited new opportunity. The story of American national growth is, in no small way, the story of the American dream's power. The American enterprise probably could not have been maintained without the American dream, because the dream provided an effective substitute for the traditional bonds of blood, region, language, class or caste, and religion which had held traditional societies together.

For on what basis could these new Americans announce so confidently, flying in the face of all the facts, that "all men are created equal"? With such divergent ethnic loyalties, and such a variety of visceral instincts for what it means to be at home, how could this overpowering land with its confusion of cultures become a homeland? How could a political system which celebrated pluralism and individualism hope to hold this polyglot population together?

Perry Miller notes that the history of American literature is the history of this continuing question: What does it mean to be an American? The American dream was as close as we have come to an answer.[4] Americans are the people who both built a better mousetrap and dreamed a grander dream, and the dream required the mousetrap. American idealism made American pragmatism a live option. The dream was the quixotic driving force that fueled the westward movement and evoked the inventive technology that made expansion practicable.

In providing a national consciousness, the American dream drew on religious themes adapted from Christianity. To be an American was to be part of a pilgrim people in covenant with a transcendent power, who had given them a promised land and a manifest destiny. The outward and visible sign of this inward and spiritual grace was the unprecedented growth and prosperity of the nation. What we now call civil religion was the substructure of the dream.[5]

From the point of view of orthodox Christian belief, civil religion is a corruption of authentic faith, because it makes its ideology a substitute for the transcendent power of the God who alone judges all things finite. From the point of view of the national community, however, civil religion is a means whereby Christianity helps provide a power for national unity that is free of traditional religion's exclusivism. In so doing, it poses a new possibility for a genuine community in a post-traditional world. In a world where traditional communities of blood, region, language, caste or class, and religion had become inextricably mixed, the Christian religion inadvertently helped provide the terms whereby an intense loyalty could be elicited from various ethnic groups, thus making "a common cake of custom" in a pluralistic and individualistic democratic society.

America's pluralistic, individualistic democracy has always lacked visible means of support. What holds this conglomerate together? Why should it work? The American Civil War was a test case. The visceral traditional bonds of blood became a fundamental issue in understanding the nature of the national enterprise. Was America to be bound by the traditional dominance of one blood community over another, or was the abstract, modern ideology of equality to prevail?

Lincoln's Gettysburg Address and Second Inaugural were definitive statements of American civil religion on this issue.[6] The notion of "the people" was to predominate and include all sorts and conditions of Americans, of whatever blood and racial group. Lord Charnwood's definitive biography of Lincoln points out that preserving the Union was more important than freeing the slaves for Lincoln because the reality of America's new pluralistic community was more significant than any specific conflict within it.

So American civil religion has had its champions, especially in the early years when the dangers of civil religion were less apparent than were its services to the nation. In the present century, however, those social critics who were at all aware of civil religion as a social force tended to be negative in their evaluation of its effect on American life. Reinhold Niebuhr was chief among them. Against the Billy Grahams and the Norman Vincent Peales, Niebuhr warned that preachers who play golf with presidents are inevitably seduced. Claiming to bring prophetic Christianity to bear on national policy, they actually cloak current national interests in the mantle of Christian piety.

Niebuhr drew the same fine line that Augustine tried to draw in the *City of God.* How can Christian faith be relevant to its social context without being co-opted by it? How can loyalty to a transcendent God remain primary while loyalty to a national community is nonetheless real? How can Christian faith be a prophetic force against injustice and, at the same time, a healing bond among divergent groups?

Niebuhr was the son of a German immigrant pastor of the Evangelical and Reformed church, and lived his early years in a Missouri community where German was still the primary language of the home, of education, and of worship. He was a pastor in suburban Detroit for thirteen years before becoming a professor of social ethics at Union Theological Seminary in New York. His career was a typically American success story: from obscurity in a rural, ethnic community that was sectarian, moralistic, and family-oriented, to world renown in an urban center that was culturally pluralistic, religiously ecumenical, morally diverse, and individualistic with a vengeance.[7]

He was fascinated with America and democracy. Tempted by the religious idealism of his immigrant youth, his experience in Detroit during the Depression and the early years of the labor movement gave him an instinctive feel for the dark side of the American dream.

Henry Ford was then paying his workers the highest hourly wage in America and crediting this generosity to Christian piety. At the same time, however, Ford laid off workers mercilessly whenever his company's profit margin narrowed. Niebuhr's later reading of Augustine on the pretensions of piety and the universality of sin gave intellectual substance to what he had already learned firsthand. He once told a student that the most formative influence on his thought had been Henry Ford.

Niebuhr championed American democracy as much for its shrewd system of checks and balances as for its idealism about human community. Our capacity for justice makes democracy possible; but our inclination to injustice makes democracy necessary. His was the prophet's task of speaking uncomfortably to the powerful, of pronouncing judgment on all forms of human pretension. He was passionately concerned to show the relevance of Christian faith to social and political life, but he was persuaded that sacrificial love or *agape*, the norm of Christian ethics, could be relevant only indirectly because social groups are inherently self-interested. A relevant Christian social ethic must be based on justice, since that is the highest achievable form of love in a sinful social world.

The high holy days of American civil religion are Memorial Day, Independence Day, and presidential inaugurals. The rhetoric of these occasions is predictably familiar and discomfiting from Niebuhr's point of view. "America is great, and can be greater still." "The future is ours if only we can emulate those heroes of our past who gave their lives for the American ideals of freedom." "The Almighty has blessed us richly with this good land, and will bless our future if we build faithfully on the sacrifices of generations past."

The message is sometimes banal, sometimes moving and lofty, but always it touches on the virtues of sacrificial love, whether Lincoln's call "that these dead shall not have died in vain," or Kennedy's that we should "ask not what your country can do for you, but what you can do for your country." This theology of sacrifice in civil religion is civil religion at its best. What Niebuhr missed most definitively in civil religion was its failure to take seriously the centrality of sacrifice in a creative human life and the severe limitations of our moral capacities. The preachers who lost their prophetic voices in the company of presidents did so because they forgot that the cross defines Christian love and that anxiety, defensiveness, and self-seeking pervert our highest ideals.

Niebuhr's Christian realism was cynical about American pieties, but compassionate about human frailty. Niebuhr found the absolutes of liberalism inhumane. It is too much to expect social groups like ethnic minorities to give over their own self-interest voluntarily out of concern for an alien and antagonistic social group. These conflicts will be resolved, he believed, partly through immediate appeals to self-interest, partly through higher appeals to social justice, and partly through legislation and social pressures that will finally give justice the force of law.

Concerned as he was for the prophetic task that both guards the sovereignty of a transcendent God and stands over against the easy conscience of popular culture, Niebuhr never went much beyond Hobbes in his understanding of the state. Nor did he give sustained attention to the positive question: Why does the American experiment work? His piecemeal, eclectic answer to that question is realistic and revealing as far as it goes, but it never quite comes to terms with the power of the dream and the radical significance of the civil religion that undergirds and informs it. He tended to regard American civil religion as a secularization of Judeo-Christian values, a golden calf which prophets of the true God must denounce. Niebuhr so influenced liberal Protestant thought on this issue that when Robert Bellah proposed a more sympathetic appraisal of American civil religion he was greated with considerable criticism.

Bellah recognized the endless possibilities for corrupting prophetic Christianity, but his focus was the perspective of the sociologist rather than the commitment of the theologian. In describing how civil religion functions in American life, he noted that it is distinct from the religion of the Christian church, but not antithetical to it. This is in marked contrast to the civil religion of the French Revolution, which was radically anticlerical and fundamentally opposed to the religious establishment. American civil religion, he noted, incorporates themes from the Christian tradition—Exodus, chosen people, Promised Land, New Jerusalem, sacrificial death and rebirth—within an American context of religious pluralism and the separation of church and state. Clearly it is not a form of theocracy, nor is it religious nationalism. Bellah insists that "American civil religion is not the worship of the American nation but an understanding of the American experience in the light of ultimate and universal reality."[8]

Although he did not explore it, Bellah opened a new possibility for understanding the theological question about God's working in history and the historical question about the impact of Christianity on world history. That possibility, that civil religion of the American type may be the effective instrument whereby Christian ideas and values become part of any culture's self-understanding, was explored by William Ernest Hocking.

Hocking and Reinhold Niebuhr are the only two American philosophers to write a philosophy of history. Hocking, in *The Coming World Civilization*,[9] agrees with Niebuhr in *The Nature and Destiny of Man* in rejecting the liberal notion of progress;[10] but Hocking argues for a pattern of meaning, nonetheless, resulting from an accumulation of historical insights, which supports Bellah's suggestion about a world civil religion.

Hocking argues that history does indeed preserve achievements. Some of these are technical. Despite the fact that certain scientific inventions have to be invented over and over again until they are finally widely known, there are certain achievements in science and technology which, once achieved, stay achieved. Hocking calls these "unlosables." The printing press, modern medical discoveries, and a host of other obvious technical examples are clearly here to stay as long as there is a human culture to employ them. Modern memory bank communications may mean that no technical achievement, however trivial, will ever again be lost—a thought which makes losability a modest value.

More important and complex are those unlosable elements that affect moral and spiritual life. Some religions disappear. Isis and Osiris are gone, even from California. In the great religions which have had such impressive longevity—who can imagine human culture without Hinduism or reverence for the Tao?—there has been considerable change, growth, and development. But certain moral and spiritual values have become inherently human, and those values have become universal.

The inherent value of the individual human being—as knower, as soul, as technical crafter of the natural world, as inherently worthy of dignity—is the chief contribution of modernity to history's store of moral and spiritual unlosables.

Democracy is the political celebration of this insight about the inherent dignity of the individual human being. It is not only historical evidence of the impact of Christian faith on the modern West; within the Christian community, it is testimony, to "eyes of faith," of the ways that God is at work in our history.[11] To be sure, those Christian enthusiasts, like Walter Rauschenbusch, who thought that they could see the Kindgom of God being established in America forgot that the Kingdom is an eschatological reality.[12] The Kingdom will be established finally only at the end of time. History is the realm of hints and guesses, of foretastes and expectations. Democracy is not the Kingdom. Democracy is only one historical foretaste of what the Kingdom may mean. It is prospect and promise, not fulfillment. It is only the intuited sense of our present historical way, not the revealed nature of our final goal.

For all that, democracy is not insignificant in the understanding of how God works in our history. The critics of democracy are always right that no democratic society fulfills the ideals of its democratic intent. As an empirical reality, it is always a question as to whether any given democratic society is more or less just than a society that does not embody democratic principles. Empirical reality is not the definitive test, however. While one flirts with the dangers of idealism in saying so, the definitive test is intention, purpose, and goal. The ground issue for any political system lies in response to the question: What does this particular national enterprise intend? Sin and self-seeking will always corrupt human enterprise, however grand. But to know what this particular people is really about, we must analyze purpose as well as performance. Democracy at its best intends to celebrate the "unlosable" value of the free individual's inherent dignity and worth.

American civil religion is the credo of America's purpose. The freedom that American life allows for expression of various beliefs also shows occasions of sacrificial care for the hopes of traditional groups other than one's own. Participants in the underground railroad of the nineteenth century, for example, are a good challenge to Reinhold Niebuhr's view that groups are not capable of sacrificial love. It followed, he argued, that national communities could not be grounded in an idea of love. Justice, he said, is the form love must take to be effective in a pluralistic society.

Niebuhr's healthy skepticism about the increasing self-interest of individuals, once they become part of large groups, made it hard for him to acknowledge ways in which the political morale of nations is often shaped definitively by the sacrificial love of communities serving a common cause. The underground railway is one of those high moments in American history that edged into the national conscience and helped define what it meant to be the kind of American that Americans have said that they intended to be.[13]

The organizers of the underground railroad were largely white people, members of the national establishment of power and influence, who were concerned that blacks obtain the freedom necessary to be a people of equal right within the national community. They put themselves at considerable risk to help people who were not in a position to do anything for them. They did it because it was the right thing to do and because they cared about the rights of those they insisted were their fellow-citizens, even though they were of a different blood community.

Events of this kind, such as the Marshall Plan, have tempted some Americans to think of these events as normative in our national life, and hence to think of themselves as a singularly good people, whom God has especially blessed, and on whose side God regularly fights. This corrupting logic, so beloved of American televangelists, is civil religion at its worst. There is no calculus for figuring whether the good America has done in the world is greater or less than the evil it has done. Events like the underground railway are evidence only that our good intentions are not always frustrated or undermined by national pride and selfishness. Yet we have a right to claim such events as an expression of who we really intend to be.

But if the biblical story means anything at all it means that chastisement and defeat are also instruments of God's work in the world. Any claim that we know God's will for us at any given time must be made in fear and trembling. No nation is exclusively God's people—God is not a tribal warlord—but some have caught a vision of loyalty to a purpose beyond their own national enterprise that is a sign of God's work to create a genuinely human community. Loyalty to the kind of democratic community that unites various traditional communities in a spirit of neighborhood is such a sign.

The significance of the American experiment in nation building is that it caught something of that vision and embodied it in its civil religion. The vision did not make it immune to retribalization of its dream, as the demonic spirit of manifest destiny made clear. The idealism of the dream has regularly been used to justify self-seeking in foreign policy and self-deception at home. Naked power-grabbing in the Mexican War and useless slaughter in Vietnam have been justified by appeals to the principles of American civil religion. In the same way, the oppression of black Americans, American Indians, and Japanese Americans during the Second World War have been obscured or justified to the national conscience by the same nationalistic appeals. The negative criticisms of American civil religion are almost always valid. It is a phenomenon fraught with demonic potential that has too often been realized.

Nor is America the beacon of the world's future, as its civil religion has too often assumed. It has been the culmination of modernity in the West, and its experiment with democracy has been widely influential. The sample of human diversity which it sought to integrate, however, was limited. In the perspective of the global village, American diversity is

relatively modest. The critical test for community building in
the postmodern world is no longer the American experiment.
That critical test is now in Eastern Europe, and especially in
the more diverse and difficult Asian experiment in community
building, which is the current task of the new India.

6

Christianity and
the New India

THE contemporary problem of building community in a
global village involves two different cultural phenomena.
On one hand is the demand of industrial collectivism in the
urban centers of Europe, North America, Australia, Japan,
and the Soviet Union, where various forms of modern individualism have created increasing social autonomy. The cultural challenge here is to maintain individualistic values while
overcoming the isolation that characterizes autonomy.

In Asia, Africa, and Latin America, on the other hand,
the problem of community develops largely out of a premodern, rural traditionalism that knows little of autonomy. Modern technology is generally welcomed in these areas, and the
younger generation celebrates the freedom from traditional
restraints promised by urbanization and modern individualistic values. The older generation, however, remembering its
rural roots in tradition, is often dismayed by the violent impact
of modernity on traditional communalism and is sometimes
able to revive traditionalism—as in present-day Iran—at least
for a time.

India is a flagship for democracy in world politics because
it is the largest and most culturally diversified modern nation

to take democracy seriously. In so doing it is dealing with these two community-building problems at the same time, having a large, modern, secular-urban, industrial society living alongside an even larger traditional religious, village, agricultural society. India's role becomes more distinctive in comparison to those new nations that call themselves democracies but have so constrained the civil rights of their citizenry as to make the notion of democracy virtually unrecognizable.

One can sympathize with the original democratic intent of several national revolutions in Latin America, for example; but no new Latin American government has demonstrated anything comparable to the political courage of India's post-independence leadership in the experiment with democratic freedoms.

Freedom of the press is always a critical test case for a genuine democracy. The Indian press is not the most sophisticated in the world, but it can be argued that it is among the freest. It can also be argued that there is no genuinely free press anywhere among the new nations in Latin America.

At the same time, no new nation anywhere can have had a better excuse for not risking a government "of the people, by the people, and for the people" than India. The Indian people are largely uneducated when not actually illiterate; and India's body politic is threatened by more radical ethnic diversity, on a larger scale, than any other contemporary nation except Russia or China—neither of which have been showcases for democratic freedoms. There are smaller nations where democracy does indeed thrive, but these nations are too culture-specific to be significant models for the pluralistic global village of the future.

The American experiment has been the fulfillment of a social and political process set in motion at the beginning of the modern period. It was not a countercurrent in modern Western culture; it came into being because it had considerable cultural momentum behind it. In India, however, the notion of a democratic political community made up of various traditional groups has faced obstacles unknown in America. The diversity of India's peoples is more radical than anything America has confronted. And while democracy in America rode the incoming tide of modern Western values, democracy in India has had to struggle against the stream of Asian traditions and their historic fatalism.

Is democracy dependent on a dominant, educated middle class, as so many argue? Or is it a global, human possibility, even in populations of illiterate, poor, agrarian villagers and peasants? The Indian experiment will have considerable weight in answering that question. If it succeeds, there will be evidence that it is possible for people of radically diverse religious and cultural backgrounds to live together in the minimal harmony necessary for a world community. If it does not succeed, there will be major additional evidence for what we always suspected: that the instinct for hate is deeper in us than the instinct for harmony; and that the prospect for human cooperation in a world community is not good.

In social and political terms India inherits and advances the American experiment with democracy. In Christian theological terms it also writes a new chapter in the story of God's community-building work in contemporary history.

The dimensions of India's task are highlighted in comparison with America's. American religious integration took place among Catholics, Protestants, and Jews; most of its major language groups were Indo-European; and the primary racial problem concerned a predominantly white population in relation to a black minority. By way of contrast, India is home to every major faith except Taoism and Confucianism and suffers a basic conflict between vegetarian Hindus on the one hand and meat-eating Muslims on the other. Linguistically, India is split three ways among the Indo-European languages of the north; the Dravidian languages of the south; and English, the language of the colonial power and therefore of government, business, and the educated middle class. Racially, India's major contrast is between the tall, thin, aquiline-nosed, brown-skinned Aryans of the north, and the shorter, more squarely built, curly-haired, darker-skinned Dravidians of the south; but northeast India also has large populations whose racial heritage is Mongol.

This cultural diversity threatens India's integrity as a national community because it is regionalized. The Indian states are organized along linguistic-cultural lines. They are centers of nascent political power, each with a fierce sense of its own identity and a long memory for the linguistic and religio-cultural history of its own community. In this sense India does not so much have a common history as it has a conglomerate of histories. The Marathas in Maharashtra remember their great leader, Shivaji; the Tamils in Tamilnad remember their own kings and poets and religious philosophers; the Sikhs in the Punjab have their own special history and identity, which has recently refocused politically; and the Kashmiris in Srinagar have always greeted travelers from New Delhi with the comment, "Ah, you have come from India."

This regional identity both makes India possible and, at the same time, threatens India's viability as a nation, since these regional identities are immediate and concrete, whereas national identity is mediated and abstract. A national identity for India, one which would supersede regional ethnic identities, requires some sort of creedal element that can appeal to the ethnic groups of the subcontinent, somehow representing the genius of each and the meaning of all. India needs its own civil religion in order to develop a binding national consciousness.[1]

Christianity has made a contribution to this national consciousness by helping to shape India's civil religion. That civil religion is grounded in Hinduism. Christianity's contribution has been to influence modern Hindu social values in a movement known variously as neo-Hinduism or the Indian renaissance, which culminated in the life and work of Mahatma Gandhi.[2]

The problem of a national self-understanding, grounded in some sort of civil religion, is illustrated by Sukarno's advocacy of *Nasakom* as the ideology of newly independent Indonesia. This faintly Muslim-based juxtaposition of nationalism, socialism, and communism was unsuccessful because it did not integrate elements already at work in the culture; rather, it superimposed on the culture a configuration of element that lacked integrity and force.

In order to understand how India has been developing an authentic and workable civil religion it is necessary to review briefly three important stages in modern Indian history: British India, the postindependence years, and some problems of the present.

The imposition of colonial rule in the early nineteenth century was not a new experience for India. Before the British there had been the Moghuls, and before them other conquerors. Some commentators have even suggested somewhat cynically that India has been great only under colonial rule. India seems to specialize in a certain resigned fatalism. India's genius is for survival, they argue, not for revolution.

Britain, however, took little note of any baseline realities in the Indian tradition. Few of Britain's colonial administrators speculated about "the real India," for British interests were primarily commercial. Commerce, however, implied an element of social philosophy that was based on the British sense of justice.

The *personae* of a commercial contract—the buyer and the seller—are abstract, generalized, faceless figures, bleached of all the vivid coloring of caste, religion, language, and region, which tradition understands as one's essential identity. In commerce, one hundred bales of Muslim cotton is precisely identical to one hundred bales of Hindu cotton, and the contract for their purchase and sale may be drawn up anywhere and in any language, by believers in any or no religion, without in any way affecting its essential nature.

Further, the contract specifies rights and privileges due to the contracting parties solely on the basis of their objective relation to the goods and services under contract. Thus the commercial contract hints at a modern conception of the individual that runs counter to traditional concepts. British law in India proceeded to make this modern concept specific.

Traditionally, the rights of the individual were limited by the immediate social group to which he or she belonged. Tradition allowed parents the right to arrange marriages for very young children without the children's consent. It denied outcastes— those who had no status in the traditional caste social structure, and who were therefore sources of pollution, or "untouchables"—access to property in most villages, since village life is regularly caste-conscious. It decreed that widows should die on the same funeral pyre with their deceased husbands. It reserved social authority and political power for royal and priestly groups, which were determined by blood and religion rather than by objective moral standards of fitness.

The legal reforms instituted in India during the days of British rule developed out of the growing conviction that there are basic, universal rights due to individuals, irrespective of birth, education, religion, color, or caste. This growing conviction was implied in the structure of British commerce, made specific by British law, and endorsed and amplified by Christian missionaries in India; but it became effective in Indian life owing to the labors of Indian reformers, from Ram Mohan Roy in the mid-nineteenth century to Mahatma Gandhi in the twentieth. Ironically, the most effective advocates of "British justice" were the Indian men and women who formed the Indian National Congress at the turn of the century. The irony was that, eventually, they insisted that the British "quit India" because the British had failed to honor the social implications of a principle they themselves had introduced into Indian life. The movement now known as neo-Hinduism or the Indian renaissance helped shape the creed of India's emerging civil religion.

Neo-Hinduism saw liberal Hindu intellectuals join forces with missionaries and colonial administrators to effect social change. The movement culminated in the thought and life of Mahatma Gandhi and was so strongly influenced by Christian ideas and values that Gandhi had to explain repeatedly that he was not a Christian. In the meantime, however, India had developed what Frantz Fanon in *The Wretched of the Earth* called a "national bourgeoisie."[3] The Indian intellectuals and business, military, and church leaders who made up the bourgeoisie were more loyal to the culture of European modernity than to the Indian tradition because they had been to Oxford or Harvard, had become Christian, or had found their place in a commercial world whose ground rules and centers of power were European. Their homes were in the modern sections of Bombay, Delhi, Calcutta, Madras, and Bangalore.

Psychologically they were split off from the culture of the Indian masses. Sometimes they were scornful of that culture, but even when sympathetic they were largely uninformed. English was not usually their mother tongue, but it was often the Indian language in which they were most fluent. They seldom visited villages. Their friendships and professional relationships were within this new urban bourgeoisie, or with Western counterparts of it.

In intellectual life, for example, Sarvepalli Radhakrishnan was comfortable as an Oxford don. In government, Jawaharlal Nehru was naturally drawn to intimate friendship with the Mountbattens. In the Indian church, many leaders shared with Western counterparts a sense of common venture and concern that was hard to duplicate among Indian peers. And in the business world, an increasing number of affluent Indians in Western business suits spent their evenings at their formerly all-British club, sipping scotch and reminiscing about grouse shooting in Scotland, or cricket matches at Lords.

For the most part, this new group knew little about traditional India. Some immersed themselves in it later in life. Aurobindo, Radhakrishnan, Gandhi, and Nehru all did this, each in his own way. Nehru confesses outright in *The Discovery of India* that, with India on the eve of independence, he knew little of its history and culture.[4] But he also makes it clear that it is no longer possible to go back. Nehru was a citizen of the new India who consciously tried to keep in touch with its past but also move beyond it.

This move was necessary for Nehru because India had made the new discovery that individuals have some rights (although it may not always be clear exactly what they are), and that these are in some sense inalienable (although plural value systems make it hard to specify just why this is true). In spite of the hindsight of gurus who announced that the Indian tradition had always prized individual rights, it was evident to Nehru that Indian values had shifted under British colonial rule. A tension had developed between tradition and modernity that would characterize the next period of Indian history.

The second period is that of the early years of Indian independence, roughly from 1947 to the death of Nehru. Independence created its own initial momentum in India, and the immediate troubles with Pakistan over Kashmir helped to sharpen India's sense that it was unified. The most telling description of India's new idea of national identity was the declaration that Indians believed in "the aims of Nehru."

Nehru came from a family of Kashmiri Brahmins. He was educated in England, first at Harrow, then at Cambridge. Perhaps he never fully understood Hindu India, but he spoke proudly and sympathetically of "our Indian heritage," and the common people sensed that he was somehow one with them. His personal charisma was enormous, and he quickly became much more than the first minister of government. Like an ancient king, Nehru *was* India. In him tradition and modernity came together.

Tamils in the south, Sikhs in the Punjab, Bengalis in Calcutta, could all believe that this national abstraction called India was real because Nehru was there to embody it for them. India was not the only newly independent nation experiencing this belief revival of virtual kingship. Sukarno in Indonesia, Nasser in Egypt, Ayub Khan in Pakistan, Nkrumah in Ghana—all were larger-than-life embodiments of the new national sense of their respective peoples. Some were good people, others not so good; but all of them were midwives of the new nationalism. Their chief function was not political programming; it was providing a symbolic unity for cultural diversity.

As long as Nehru was on the scene, India would be India. But toward the end of his life the question was asked, "After Nehru, what?" A nation cannot be built overnight. Along with a creed that expresses national purpose, time is needed in order to forge a common history and to make those commitments in education, commerce, and the arts that bind disparate cultural elements into a community.

At Nehru's death it was clear that there had not been enough time. Shastri's leadership was all too brief, and the ruling Congress party turned to Indira Gandhi in the hope that she might have inherited some of her father's charisma. The Gandhi government initiated the third period of contemporary Indian history. The national unity built up during the struggle for independence had begun to erode visibly. The gods of history seem disposed to give each newly independent nation a birthday gift of one parental figure to help ease cultural conflicts; but after that the nation is left on its own.

Suharto was not Sukarno, nor could Nehru's daughter be expected to play the role her father played for India. The defeat of her son Rajiv marked the end of the Nehru era in Indian politics as a new pluralism emerged. India's language problem is not resolved, however, and Hindi may never be widely used as a national language in the south. Religious conflict between Hindus and Muslims continues. The political power of the states grows; regionalism is strengthened. The Sikh autonomy movement, while not unique in postindependence India—the Tamils in the south and Kashmiris in the north have both tried it—has been powerfully militant. And the conflict between Tamils and Sinhalese in Sri Lanka—not to mention internal conflicts between various groups from the same ethnic background—threatens India's future. So it is neither cynical nor melodramatic to wonder whether the Indian nation will survive as it is presently constituted.

There have always been knowledgeable and not unfriendly observers who had their doubts as to that survival, noting that British India was initially a commercial structure that became politically viable only through considerable military force. The political unity of British India was a superstructure that was not determined by the internal politics of India's chronically contentious sociopolitical regions.

Modern India was originally an artificial product manufactured in the British Foreign Office. And Britain was marvelously equipped for governance. It possessed a rich linguistic heritage in English, which is infinitely adaptable to the terminological requirements of modern science; a tight-knit national pride and loyalty so fierce it often seemed to parody Gilbert and Sullivan; a gift for unsentimental and sometimes brutal practicality; a disciplined army and a long tradition of overseas administrative expertise; and a common religious commitment that readily identified God's will with the national interest and lent considerable strength, clarity, and purpose to Britain's adventures in empire. In short, it was easier in many ways for the British to administer the government of India than it was for indigenous Indian political parties.

Since independence, India's government has been committed to democratic socialism and secularism. Under the heading of democratic socialism it seeks to establish a society based on a fundamental conception of human rights and government responsibility for the needs of all citizens, although its economic successes have owed much to indigenous capitalism. Under the heading of secularism it refuses to base the idea of human rights on any particular religion, and therefore, in effect, rejects traditionalism in India.

At the same time, however, India requires something of the force of religious conviction to make this new understanding capable of withstanding what Shastri called the "fissiparous forces" of regional contentiousness. Nehru's appeal to a vague Indian mystique located somewhere in the Indian tradition was therefore a realistic necessity for Indian democracy. But a credo for the new India cannot be made up out of whole cloth. Unless the process of social and political modernization maintains its links with tradition, the national bourgeoisie will lose touch with the villagers, and there will be no total transformation of Indian society.

The experience of contemporary Iran is instructive in relation to India's search for a sense of national unity. Mansour Farhang, revolutionary Iran's first ambassador to the United Nations, argues that the Islamic revolution was a success—to everyone's surprise, including both the American C.I.A. and the Ayatollah Khomeini—because the urban poor were more concerned with reclaiming their traditional identity than they were with the immediate daily necessities of food and shelter. The modernization program of the Shah had neither included them nor given them a sense of belonging in the national community. The ayatollahs did not give them bread; they gave them stony sermons. But the urban poor gave the ayatollahs their loyalty and made the revolution a success.[5]

On the face of it, there is no apparent reason why democratic societies should succeed. Take people of varied ethnic backgrounds; tell them that they are all equal and have equal rights, especially the right to numerous heady freedoms; and then ask, Why should they make common cause? There is no very good answer to this question from the storehouse of self-interest, apart from the minimal need to be protected from harassment. But even those huddled together against the storm of common danger will not move forward without some idea of goal and purpose. The proponents of *realpolitik* are probably half right; greed and self-interest explain part of such decisions. But greed and self-interest do not explain loyalty, or why people care about a cause, often at great cost to themselves, even at the cost of their lives.

In *The Discovery of India*, Nehru noted that India's cultural continuity had been rooted in three major social forces: caste, the autonomous village, and the joint family. But in the new India, urbanization, modernization, and democratization are gradually eroding them all. So where does Nehru find the "binding ingredient" of the new India? He is vague, not unlike his American counterparts in their celebration of the American dream. He speaks of India as a "sentiment . . . [which] went far back into the remote periods of Indian history." He also speaks of it as a "conflict . . . between two approaches to the

problem of social organization, which are diametrically opposed to each other; the old Hindu conception of the group
being the basic unit of organization, and the excessive individualism of the West, emphasizing the individual above the
group."[6]

Somehow, he suggests, there must be a melding of these
two, with religion, philosophy, and science interrelated. He
notes: "We can never forget the ideals that have moved our
race, the dreams of the Indian people through the ages, the
wisdom of the ancients, the buoyant energy and love of life
and nature of our forefathers. . . . We will never forget them
or cease to take pride in that noble heritage of ours."[7] But
how do ancient religious and philosophical values meld with
modern scientific and industrial ones?

On one level the answer is that they do it willy-nilly, by
coexisting long enough so that they reach some rough, workable, instinctive accommodation with one another. Every all-
India institution—the government of India, the army, the universities, large corporations, and the like—engenders over
time just such an accommodation of values, and in so doing
helps to shape a new national consciousness. In the early years
of national independence this accommodation tended to be
somewhat schizophrenic, however, and limited to the experience of the leadership class.

The public life of this new Indian middle class, including
social and professional relations within the peer group, tends
toward modern values of individualism and scientific thought
because these pan-Indian institutions are modern. In their
private lives and familial relations, however, these same people tend to maintain many of their old religious and philosophical instincts, values, and persuasions.

As middle-class urban life becomes more modern, this
class becomes further removed from the rural life of the mass
of Indian villagers. This socioeconomic problem has been
widely noted and much discussed. Less obvious, but equally
important, is the personal and spiritual problem of people in

this leadership class as they sense a certain inner alienation from themselves. They are not "at home." Having two sets of values and living in two different worlds is at best discomfiting. Granted, life under the Raj made many a middle-class Indian adept at living in two worlds. Nirad Chaudhuri, the ageless *enfant terrible* of Indian letters, even suggests that the Janus model is indigenous to Hinduism.[8] Even so, one cannot be at home in the new India without finally being at home with oneself. So the political search for civil loyalty, grounded in a civil religion, is related to the spiritual search for a measure of inner personal integrity.

One possible solution to this dilemma on the part of the Hindu majority in India is to follow the theocratic lead of those neighbors like Pakistan and reconceive the Indian experiment as Hindusthan. The power of such "fundamentalist" appeal lies partly in the restoration of inner spiritual integrity, not only for the middle class, but also for the urban poor. This appeal was noted prominently in Farhang's analysis of Khomeini's victory in the Iranian revolution. But it is now, happily, too late for that in India, if the Indian experiment in secular democracy is to survive.

This is not to say that the Hindu fundamentalists may not win out in the end. It is only to say that, if they do, fissiparousness will be the order of the day, civil war will be the common plight of India's ethnic groups, political balkanization will result, and the dreams of both Nehru and Gandhi will have died. In Nehru's fine phrase, India will no longer be India. And the rest of the world will have to turn elsewhere for a model serving the coming world civilization.

When Nehru spoke of forces that could provide India with a common goal, purpose, and identity, he clearly had something more in mind than the pragmatic influences of India's modern urban institutions. Almost half of the brief epilogue to *The Discovery of India* is given to an account of Emerson's Harvard speech on "The American Century," which was a plea to Americans to focus their intellectual attention on

American culture rather than on the culture of Europe.[9]

Here Nehru seems to sense an "Indian Century" in the making. He pleads for a focus on India's cultural heritage. He bemoans the decline in Indian culture that lasted into the nineteenth century and calls for a revival of ideas and values that are indigenously Indian. But he pays relatively little attention to the Indian renaissance, which began with the reform work of Ram Mohan Roy and culminated in the influence of Gandhi and Nehru himself. That development, stimulated by British colonial rule, modern scientific education, and the Christian missionary movement, both revived and revised a distinctive Indian spirituality that is now a crucial element in Indian civil loyalty. It also provides a significant example of how Christian life and thought can serve the civil religion of a non-Christian culture. The story of neo-Hinduism is, in part, the story of the "christianization" of Hinduism, not in terms of theological convictions, but in regard to ethical values and practices, based on a new sense of the dignity of the individual human being.[10]

The significance of this movement was real but modest. It was largely limited to an early group of Hindu middle-class intellectuals and reformers. Their major interreligious interaction was with the Serampore missionaries and their successors who represented Western religious values and ideas. It was by no means a pan-Indian movement, and its continuing influence is uncertain. Nevertheless, it was one cultural development in modern India that clearly reclaimed elements of India's cultural heritage and fitted those elements for service to the New India.

That, of course, was the task that a developing civil religion faced. Was it possible, somehow, to "decontextualize" some creative elements of the Indian religious tradition and make those elements available to modern urban middle-class people, as well as the urban poor and the mass of villagers, in a form that could maintain its spiritual power while shedding its exclusivist religious context?

Was it possible both to modernize and "Indianize" critical elements in the religious and cultural context that had previously been traditional, fissiparous, exclusivist, and antinational?

What would be required is a "binding ingredient" that would also function as a "load-lifting idea," a notion of national meaning and purpose that would help overcome the burdens of cultural inferiority, economic inadequacy, and religious irrelevance which colonialism imposed on the Indian spirit.[11] Such a formula of national meaning for a democratic society with India's radical cultural pluralism must be more than cultural nostalgia. It must be "creedal" in some sense. That is, it must celebrate some values in which people believe, some virtues which, by transcending nationalism, create "brotherhood" and "sisterhood," both for the nation and for the larger human community.

So, for example, "freedom" to establish a government "of the people, by the people, and for the people" became the principal doctrine of the American creed. What is the principal doctrine of the Indian creed? Nehru did not seem to move beyond nostalgia, at least not in *The Discovery of India*. Nor did he seem to be aware that he was part of a neo-Hindu movement that presented a coherent theme, from the early reforms of Ram Mohan Roy to the independence struggle led by Gandhi and himself.

The leading figures of this Indian renaissance—from Ram Mohan Roy, Keshub Chander Sen, the Tagores, Aurobindo, Sri Ramakrishna, and Swami Vivekananda down to Gandhi and Nehru—shared the conviction that Indian spirituality had a special contribution to make to the world. The message of Rabindranath Tagore's *Toward Universal Man*, shared by others in this movement, was central. Tagore argued that India's experience of cultural diversity had given it a special insight into tolerance and that the rationale for that tolerance is the common humanity that we all share.[12] This idea features in the work of each major reformer in this movement.

With Roy it was an openness to common cause with the
missionaries to oppose *sati* (widow burning), along with his
own conviction that the spiritual tolerance of the Hindu tradition must now be joined with a new social concern in defense
of human rights. With Keshub it was a religious openness to
various views which were to be institutionalized in the
Brahmo Samaj, a modern Hindu "church" that borrowed
much from Christian Unitarianism. Hinduism had not traditionally been an institution; it had been a culture and a
personal persuasion. The worshippers at a given temple were
not an organized community like a Christian congregation,
nor were there institutional links among various Hindu tem-
ples. Now, with a new focus on social responsibility, neo-
Hinduism turned toward institutionalization in order to become an effective social force. The most striking and lasting
example of this institutionalization is the Ramakrishna Mission, which established social welfare programs, promoted
modernized Hindu thought, and, through the genius and energy of Swami Vivekananda, became a missionary movement
in the West as well as in India.

With Aurobindo it was a view of the new Hindu as transcendental, a "Gnostic Being" empowered with an unprecedented universality, capable of living The Life Divine.[13] But
even this was not the old asocial transcendentalism of traditional Hinduism, for Aurobindo had been a political activist
who had founded the global village of Auroville, a community
reminiscent of the American Puritans' "city set upon a hill,
for all the world to see." It was to be a model for a new world
community, including all sorts and conditions of folk from
every nation, and containing patches of soil taken from all
the countries of the world. It was not widely influential, but
the intent it embodied was characteristic of this movement.

With Ramakrishna Paramahamsa, Swami Vivekananda,
and the founding of the Ramakrishna Mission, however, the
movement became more than pan-Indian and achieved international influence. Vivekananda became a world figure. He
gave a widely noted speech at the Congress of World Religions

in Chicago in 1897, was offered professorships in philosophy at two major American universities, and returned home in triumph, celebrating the theme of *ex oriente lux*, in contrast to the century-old colonialist/missionary theme that the West was the bearer of light while the East was an area of darkness. For Vivekananda the idea of "tolerance" was no longer a defense against Western cultural encroachments in India; it was now a battle cry of creative insight into the spiritual power that was making India strong again.

This new notion of tolerance has, I think, become the load-lifting idea providing a binding ingredient among India's various cultural groups. It is the idea that best summarizes Nehru's ruminations on what makes India truly India. It is not the old transcendental, Stoic aloofness with its disregard for the historical world of society and culture because it is *prakṛti* ("nature") or *māyā* ("illusion"), whereas the inner world of *puruṣa* ("spirit") or *ātman* ("soul/self") is the world that really matters.

The Indian renaissance turned that transcendentalism in a historic direction—aided by the twin influences of "British justice" and the social concern of the missionaries—so that the old schizophrenia between the intolerance of a caste-ridden society and the universal acceptance of all in *Brahma* was gradually overcome. The new tolerance argued that, since it is spiritual, it must also be social, and that without that equation, the idea lacks integrity.

Gandhi continues to be the key figure in this development, and his genius is nowhere more evident than in his reinter-pretation of the idea of *ahiṃsā*, "nonviolence." The only pre-modern use of *ahiṃsā* in a *social* context was by Ashoka in the third century B.C., and then only after considerable blood-shed.[14] Gandhi, however, almost succeeded in persuading an entire nation that this notion was the meaning of who they had always been. Gandhi himself, devastated by the com-munal riots that accompanied partition, died convinced that he had failed. But his reinterpreted doctrine of *ahiṃsā* may yet prove to be a success, not because India turns out to be more tolerant, in a nonviolent way, than other national communities, but because India makes the nonviolent, tolerant way the goal and purpose that it serves.[15]

Here pragmatism is strained, and the temptation to revert to the old irrelevant, idealistic transcendentalism becomes acute. Nevertheless, one must ask whether Americans are more free than others for whom freedom is not the specific load-lifting idea that binds their national community together. It is dangerous to say that intent is more important than achievement, but in the matter of civil religion that is the case, as long as the distance between the two is not too great. In these matters, reach always exceeds grasp, but creative interchange requires proximity.

Tolerance, in this complex sense, is no longer exclusively Hindu; but it is distinctively Indian. *Swaraj* ("freedom"), for example, as an outgrowth of this idea, is quite different from the American notion of freedom because of the special quality of Indian tolerance and universality. America's freedom is feisty and contentious. Gandhi's revision of *ahiṃsā* drenches Indian notions of freedom with a spirit of nonviolence that the early American patriot Patrick Henry ("Give me liberty, or give me death") would have found anathema. For Patrick Henry and most Americans, the fight for freedom means the willingness to die in the struggle to kill the opponent in order to win the day. For Gandhi, on the other hand, the fight for freedom means a commitment to convert the opponent, at the risk of being killed by him or her, but never to kill. These are different worlds of thought and action.

Nehru, celebrating "the ideas that have moved our race," includes his forebears' "toleration of ways other than theirs, their capacity to absorb other peoples and their cultural accomplishments, to synthesize them and develop a varied and mixed culture." These values, he says, "lie embedded in our subconscious minds," and "if India forgets them she will no longer remain India."[16]

Civil religion is less concerned with the past than with the future; it is concerned less with accomplishment than with goal and intention. Always vague and visceral, it provides self-definition by commitment to a goal. Whether Indians are actually more tolerant than others is not as much the point as whether tolerance and universality are what India has chosen to stand for.

The Indian renaissance articulated an understanding of what it means to be an Indian, and the significance of that achievement for India's political future is considerable. The "fissiparous tendencies" of traditional groups continue to threaten balkanization. That tendency will not be countered by a politics of fear, or self-interest, or inertia alone. The binding ingredient of India's civil religion, the idea that will lift the load of colonialism, is also necessary and makes a contribution not only to Indian unity but to the larger prospect for world peace among peoples of different and antagonistic ethnic and religious backgrounds.

Christianity contributed substantially to making the classic passive notion of tolerance into an active principle of social justice and reform. That contribution was recognized by Hindu leaders like Sarvepalli Radhakrishnan, who objected to missionary proselytizing, but who repeatedly celebrated "the missionary spirit" of social service. Christianity also learned something about its own proclamation from the newly developed notion of Hindu tolerance. Gandhi's reinterpretation of *ahiṃsā* gave Martin Luther King, Jr., a new understanding of the meaning of Christian love as *agape*, and a social method of nonviolent resistance for expressing that commitment.

India provides evidence that Christianity can help community building in non-Christian cultures through its contribution to civil religion. But the history of Christianity in India also gives evidence that the Christian proclamation is often insensitive to the realities of life and belief in other religious cultures, and therefore results in community destroying rather than community making. If Christian ideas and values are to serve the cause of a genuinely human community, Christians must learn to think and speak in a new way.

Part III

Part III

7

Thinking in a New Way:
The Problem of Power

MODERNITY destroyed the cohesiveness of the medieval world, and with it the hold Christianity had on Western culture. While the content of the new culture was an affirmation of individualism in economics, religion, politics, science, and the humanities, the dominant authority of the new culture was not a specific content but the experimental method of the new empirical sciences.[1]

Following the Roman thrust into northern Europe, the energies of the High Middle Ages had turned toward cultural consolidation and intellectual coherence. The individualistic spirit of modernity, however, was a spirit of exploration and adventure. The hallmark of medieval intelligence had been the integrative capacity for system. The critical intelligence of modernity, on the other hand, was revolutionary.

From Descartes onward, the philosophic and scientific prize was won by those who could conceive of things differently. Newton, Darwin, and Einstein all proposed integrating systems of thought, but their genius lay in their capacity to find a new point of departure for a world view.

Christian theology was sometimes partner in these outbursts of cultural imagination. The Copernican revolution was informed by certain theological persuasions, and the rise of capitalism was energized by the spirit of Protestantism. But the substance of these new world views was no longer self-consciously theological. The Christian church continued to be a major institution of modern culture, but increasingly it was one institution among many.

The politics of democracy characteristically insisted on a separation of church and state. Even when democracy included a relation to an established church, that relationship was increasingly formal. Modernity challenged the Christian church with an increasingly subordinate role as a cultural institution, and the postmodern world now adds the challenge of cultural and religious pluralism.

Some Christian theologians have argued that secularization actually extended the meaning of the Christian faith. *The Secular City*[2] by Harvey Cox and *The Secular Meaning of the Gospel*[3] by Paul van Buren suggest that secularity was itself a notion informed by significant elements of the Christian faith, and that the secular world was a resource for Christian living and not a threat to Christian meanings. This view was a reaction to the emphasis on transcendence in much Protestant neoorthodox theology[4] and a reaffirmation of the liberal notion that Christian thought illuminates the meaning of life and is not a system of ideas and values superimposed on human experience from a privileged position of authority.

In a somewhat different vein, William Ernest Hocking in *The Coming World Civilization* argued that the secularization of the West freed Christianity from its tie to Western thought and institutions and made its universal applicability to the human situation increasingly apparent.[5] Echoing Augustine's view that Christian faith is the natural religion of humankind, Hocking argued that Christianity's parenting of Western cultural institutions had become a liability in a planetary world, and that secularization made possible a new understanding of the Christian world mission.

While they were overly optimistic about the spiritual depth of a secular society, these books were belated reminders that the church's triumphal predominance in Western culture was always something of an embarrassment to Christian life and faith. Conceived as a message of hope for aliens, pilgrims, and outsiders, the notion of mastery in this world never conjoined with the more profound and winsome graces of the Christian way.

There was always something fundamentally bizarre about crosses on the banners of kings. For people whose primary loyalty was to a Kingdom not of this world, identity with the aims and purposes of any state was a sign of corruption. The conversion of Constantine was not necessarily a denial of the Christian ethos, but it created a profound ambiguity in subsequent Christian self-understanding. Most perplexing was the problem of power.

Jesus' exhortation to render unto Caesar the things that were Caesar's, his insistence that the poor were blessed, and his alienation from both civil and religious authority made it clear that his followers were not to seek power as the world understood it. Let Caesar have his authority; let the rich have their money; let the priests have their doctrinal control. They have their reward. The way of faithfulness to God was not concerned with this kind of power. On the other hand, power of a different sort was clearly at the heart of the new gospel, and was not purely spiritual.

The power to move mountains through faith, the power to make the lame walk and the blind see, the power to make the dead live—this power was not otherworldly as opposed to worldly; nor was it spiritual as opposed to political. It was self-giving rather than self-seeking. To be a Christian was to seek power *for* other people, to confer power *on* them, rather than to seek power *over* them. And the power that one sought to confer was not political or financial or even religious. In keeping with the historic Christian emphasis on the freedom and dignity of the individual human being, it was primarily personal power. It was the power to be one's God-given self. It was the power of Christ for the salvation of one's soul, as part of the soul of the community. The Christian call was to serve the community of humankind. Servanthood, not mastery, was the touchstone of the Christian way.

Reassessment of power requires some theme of interpretation to understand why modern social and institutional structures are no longer creative, and what alternative characteristics a Christian movement serving human community must adopt. Such themes of reflection are never precise, and are always misleading if taken too seriously. They function as symbols, ways of grasping broad, amorphous issues. The outlines of the problem are increasingly clear, however.

In the modern West an autonomous culture prized virtues that enhanced the control of nature, the exploration of uncharted regions, and the development of new economic systems, a high technology, and, eventually, a system of unimaginably powerful military weapons. These virtues centered in a creative imagination that could conceive how the world might be different—the hallmark of modern intelligence—and an aggressive energy geared to shaping and controlling the environment to embody that imaginative conception.

The virtues that the new world community now most needs are those enabling values that can help us to overcome the individual isolation of our autonomy and to reestablish a holistic integration of ourselves with others and with the world of nature. This is not to say that one set of virtues is superior to the other, but only that "new occasions teach new duties" as the old hymn puts it, and that "time makes ancient good uncouth." Modernity was a creative move beyond the constraints of traditional society, but modern autonomy threatens to self-destruct without readmitting some of the virtues of its old antithesis.

An age develops its virtues in response to its tasks. Modernity's task called forth a celebration of freedom, individuality, courage, and practical imagination. These virtues of a "hard" or "linear" creativity are more aggressive than receptive, more adventuring than enabling, focused on the individual more than on the community. The virtues of a "soft" or "holistic" creativity are inclusive rather than exclusive, synthetic rather than analytic, ontological rather than technical.

This last distinction is the most significant, because it touches an autonomous culture's longing for a traditional home. That loss is the ontological connection to the community, provided especially by bonds of blood, but also by identity with the symbols of soil or region, language, caste or class, and religion. The rediscovery of our community with others and with nature requires a renewed emphasis on the significance of "ontological" reason, as opposed to purely "technical" reason.

In the traditional villages of Tamilnad in South India today, for example, one does not say "I speak Tamil" or "I live in Tamilnad" (Tamil Country) as though these were choices that individuals had made from among several options. One cannot *become* Tamil; one *is* Tamil. Tamil is the nature of one's *being*. One's Tamil identity is ontological. And when one says "I am Tamil," this identification includes a language, a region, a network of blood connections, caste groupings, and religious traditions.

The transformation of autonomy, therefore, not only involves the reintegration of traditional society's holistic virtues with modernity's linear ones. It also requires a way of thinking and understanding oneself and one's community that is ontological as well as technical. This new way of thinking will combine elements from both tradition and modernity. This remaking of the postmodern mind is necessary if there is to be a genuine human community.

The classical Greek philosophy of Aristotle understood cause as having not only material and efficient dimensions, but formal and final ones. And the final cause is its purpose in being that kind of thing. The technical reason developed after the Cartesian revolution in philosophy focused on the material and efficient causes of a thing, and regarded the formal cause nominalistically as an arbitrary name rather than an ontological kind. Perhaps most significantly, modern technical reason dropped the notion of final cause altogether. "Things" in the modern world do not participate in the structure of reason; they are only reasoned about. To have a final purpose, however, is to be grounded in the structure of intelligibility that gives the world of nature and society its coherence.

Technical reason is reason as instrument or tool.[6] It is necessarily narrow in conception in order to achieve a limited but vital universality. For all the differentiation of human notions about what is true, we can all agree that $2 + 2 = 4$; that kind of common rational ground is a precious human achievement as well as an implement for fashioning human ends. In dealing with a universe of the empirically verifiable, technical reason allows us to weigh and measure with astounding sophistication.

Technical reason per se, however, tells us nothing of values, whether moral or aesthetic; and it yields no ultimate meanings, whether personal, spiritual, or religious. Because modern culture has been absorbed in the conquest of physical nature, technical reason has gained enormous prestige. But that prestige has made it extremely difficult for philosophy to deal adequately with issues of meaning, which do not yield readily to quantification and control. Further, technical reason has tended to be exclusive, rather than inclusive. It has sometimes left the ontology of meaning and value in a philosophic wilderness. The result has been epistemological schizophrenia.

The most vivid recent example of this split mindset is the retrospective account of physicists who worked on the Manhattan Project to build the atom bomb and who now lecture against development of atomic weapons. Technical reason presupposes that truth—any truth, all truth—is the definitive scientific virtue. Learning something new, anything new, about the world and its workings is self-justifying for technical reason and the culture of liberalism which celebrated it. Pure science seeks objective truth for its own sake, and the inevitable result will be human progress.

Against this ideology built on technical reason, any individual scientist's moral uncertainty must have seemed puny and irrelevant. The project was too compelling; the evil of

Hitler too obvious; and the relevance of personal ethical concern too tenuous. So the "scientist" tends to become separate from the "person" doing the science. And reason in such a situation is no longer the function of a humane intelligibility in an integrated world view. Reason is now a free-floating instrument available for any investigation that a political and economic climate can sustain.

Concern over the problem of how we know other minds than our own is another example.[7] Philosophers as individual people have not personally doubted that other philosophers also had minds, in the same sense that they know themselves to have minds. The prestige of technical reason had been so great, however, that some have concluded that their own deepest assurance on this matter lacks the status of genuine knowledge. The effect is insidious, persuading people to deny their own experience in favor of a misplaced abstraction.

Inevitably, there has been a countercurrent in modernity as evidenced in romanticism, in depth psychology, in the theology of feeling, and, most notably, in existentialism. The philosophies of religion, art, society, and the self have dealt seriously with the relations among myth, symbol, and reality; the persistence of value; the inexplicable motivations of individual selves; and the dynamics of social interactions. In various movements—process thought, phenomenology, existentialism, comparative philosophy, feminist thought—philosophy has begun a rapprochement between technical reason and classical or ontological reason.

These movements have been occasioned by a crisis in the prestige of a purely technical reason. In denying the status of knowledge to the moral and spiritual assurances of human experience, the personally insidious prestige of such an extreme form of technical reason becomes culturally dangerous. Because it is only a tool, cut loose from the structure of rationality in the total range of one's experienced world, technical reason too easily falls prey to manipulation by the forces of irrationality. The philosophic debate over the "other minds problem" is only a conundrum in a specialized academic discipline. The technocracy of Nazi Germany, however, is a tragedy in which technical reason became a tool of demonic retribalization in modern society. The elaborate rationales of Aryan ideology overruled the instinctive moral and spiritual values of a sophisticated culture.

To reappropriate soft creativity into modernity's hard creativity is to reassess the values of traditional society. The danger of this reassessment is the destructive possibility of retribalization if these two types of creativity are not appropriately balanced. The fundamental human yearning for community in which people of common blood, region, language, caste or class, and religion are drawn to their own kind, and fear those who are strangers, is subject to two forms of unbalanced, destructive irrationality. One of these is technical, the other ontological.

When technical reason combines with traditional natural bonds of blood, region, language, caste or class, and religion, the result is a hard irrationality, such as the Aryanism of Nazi Germany, the tribalism of Idi Amin's Uganda, or the fundamentalism of Khomeini's Iran. When ontological reason combines with nostalgia for the sense of being at home, the result is the soft irrationality of the Transcendentalist commune of Brook Farm or the hippie communes of the sixties.

While there is much to be learned from the intimacy of the preindustrial village and the holistic meanings of tribal living, especially its sense of unity with nature, we are well rid of their prejudices, superstitions, and constraints; nor could we return if we chose. The seductiveness of soft irrationality works like a dry rot from within, sapping energies, enveloping facts in a cloud of fantasy, floating idealism far enough from its moorings to rob it of cash value in the daily round.

Conjoining these values is a task for the creative imagination of a characteristically modern intelligence that can conceive how things might be different from how they have been in the past. This way of thinking is alien to the traditional mind. Traditionalism has no gift for novelty. It is, ironically, the characteristic capacities of a hard creativity which make the reappropriation of a soft creativity possible.

One of the most critical issues for the movement toward community is the problem of power. We need a new understanding of power as enabling, as well as controlling. The psychology of control assumes that the controller knows how the controlled should behave, and that the controlled has no purpose or the wrong purpose. In shaping physical nature to human purposes, control was regularly creative. Rampant floods and rampant viruses are irrational evils. Our current ecological crisis, however, results from the hubris of technical reason disregarding the wisdom of nature. Ontological reason by itself has no gift for this necessary technical control, but it has an instinctive trust of natural process. It assumes a measure of wisdom in nature because it regards nature as participating in the structure of rationality.

Industrial efforts to curb pollution are still widely regarded as controls, but they involve the belated recognition that our air and water are meant to be clean, for a good reason. Modern medicine has sought to control disease by therapies that are largely invasive. The recent experiments in holistic medicine temper these controls with a renewed trust in the body's own instinct for health, and employ natural therapies that enable that process. Even the concept of organization is now subject to experiments with power as enabling rather than controlling.

Modern industrial organization has been largely hierarchical and mechanical, with power effected from the top, to be implemented by lower-level management. The assignment of lower-level tasks in such a structure is as specific as possible, implying only minimal trust of those assigned to perform them. Recent experiments with "matrix management" and decentralized organization are allowing greater responsibility and the exercise of purposeful imagination at lower levels, thereby enhancing organizational morale and often increasing productivity. And in the organization of family life, the notion that each household has a head, responsible for final decision making, is now often tempered with the realization that families are cooperative systems that become dysfunctional without sharing of responsibilities and appropriate mutual respect.

Community, however, requires a cultural transformation that not only employs new techniques but also is grounded in a renewal of fundamental belief. Community assumes respect and care for the other, in spite of our cultural and religious differences, and a conviction about the inherent human rights and dignity of all people. A barbarian is one to whom we must explain why this is so; and barbarism is on the rise.

The Christian faith no longer controls the fundamental convictions of Western culture from a position of institutional power. To that extent it is freed from the anachronism of preaching the power of enablement while exercising the power of control.

The Christian story is shot through with the paradox of worldly weakness revealed as spiritual strength. Its message is that only in losing one's life does one find it; and its only power is the power of God for salvation. Its task is to feed the hungry, clothe the naked, comfort the bereaved, and proclaim the Kingdom. But its message is not just for the community of Christian believers. It is for the human community, because it is not only a proclamation about what we are called to. It is also a revelation of how, in fact, things are with us.

The fullness of that revelation is bound to the mystery of faith in Jesus Christ as Lord. But the social and political impact of that faith is not bound to its fullness. The engagement of the institutional church with any given culture gives rise to movements in which Christian people make common cause with people of different religious persuasions and social and ethnic backgrounds. These movements engage directly in programs of social reform and political action in which the institutional church, as such, cannot engage. The moral and spiritual convictions of their particular backgrounds motivate each participant, but the morale of their common venture is enabled by a common loyalty to the cause they serve.

Civil religion, therefore, is not necessarily a corruption of Christian faith just because it does not represent the fullness of faith. Only from a sectarian and triumphalist point of view must civil religion be necessarily regarded as a corruption of the Christian proclamation. On the national level—and the critical political reality in our world is the nation—civil religion is loyalty to the cause of the community.

Community does not require cultural and religious homogeneity. It is rather a context in which various religious and cultural traditions can deepen their own belief structures, in conversation with one another. It is a context in which religious difference is no longer fearsome to the point where Protestants will fight their neighbors because they are Catholic, or Hindus slaughter their neighbors because they are Muslim. Community is evident in the soft, vague, but persistent sense that my God and my neighbor's God are not two different controlling powers in our common universe, but one enabling and sustaining power that we all struggle to know more fully and serve more faithfully. The reintegration of ontological reason into modernity's technical reason makes it possible to articulate some value-laden ideas that can be shared across different cultures and religions. Community then enables the most cherished of all human hopes—the hope for peace.

8

Speaking in a New Way: Overcoming Fear of the Other

RELIGIOUS thought is always culturally conditioned. Christianity believes that Jesus, the Christ, is "the same yesterday, today, and forever"; but Christian thought about Jesus changes from generation to generation, because Christianity is a historical religion. Each generation must ask Dietrich Bonhoeffer's question: "Who is Christ for us today?" Hence Christian thought regularly reexamines the Bible, the history of the church, and the history of culture in order to rediscover God's work in the present.

Until recently Christian thought has been largely a Western cultural enterprise, and in keeping with the controlling spirit of that culture, Christian thought has been "apologetic," that is, its persuasive argument has intended a change of mind and heart in those addressed.

Philosophical argument had three significant functions for the early church.[1] It helped to clarify the meaning of basic Christian ideas, such as the trinitarian nature of God. It helped defend Christian orthodoxy, thus established, from the heretical or heterodox views of Gnostics, Arians, and others. And it helped persuade those outside the church of the truth of the Christian faith. It was this last use of argument which came to the fore in shaping modern Christian theology.

After the High Middle Ages, Christianity was increasingly on the defensive, both in regard to the scientific humanism of its own culture and in regard to other world religions. Christian theology presented itself in both its Catholic and Protestant forms as a world view with metaphysical intent. Even when it eschewed the niceties of logic or rejected philosophy as an authority, it was nonetheless intending to propose a reasonable view of who we are, what our world is like, and who is ultimately the author and sustainer of the human adventure. And it was increasingly pressured, by the secularization of modern society, to defend itself.

The defensive-aggressiveness of this enterprise was sharpened by the principle of noncontradiction which Aristotle had made a cornerstone of Western logic. The principle stated that a thing cannot both be and not be in the same way at the same time. Applied to religious truth claims, the principle required exclusivism. In dealing with other world religions, Christian thought suffered much confusion between the requirements of its culture's logic and the spirit of its religion's Lord.

The logic of persuasive argument has been so closely identified with Christian evangelism and the affirmation of the Christian world mission that it is unthinkable to many that Christian faith could maintain its integrity apart from willingness to make those exclusive truth claims that have characterized modern Christian evangelism. But this proselytizing use of persuasive argument is a form of power as control over other people, relying more heavily on the hard rationality of technical reason than on the soft rationality of ontological reason. It has been fraught with fear of the other. Even discovery that we share common ground with believers in other religions initially promotes fear. Our instinctive response is to deny the validity of the other's understanding of "our" religious idea, lest we gradually lose our own religious identity.

That kind of anxiety negates its own conviction, however. To trust the God who is revealed in Jesus, the Christ, is not to believe in the accuracy of certain rational propositions of technical reason about him. It is rather to trust that the truth of God's presence in him will work its way in all cultures so that both Christians and non-Christians will discover new truth. If Christian thought is to participate in a postmodern transition to a humane world culture, the structure of its thought must reflect its commitment to God's power of enablement, even in alien contexts, and must reappropriate the soft rationality of ontological reason with increasing emphasis on imagination, mystery, and the intimate relation between feeling and idea.

What is now called "story theology" moves in this direction, but story theology too often assumes that myths and symbols have universal meanings that supersede abstract philosophical formulation.[2] However, this is usually not the case. To an American from Massachusetts, for example, *ocean* means Cape Cod, swimming, clipper ships, Moby Dick, and all those other familiar symbols resulting from its recreational uses and its rich maritime history. In India, on the other hand, where very few people know how to swim, and where there is little maritime history but a rich legacy of religious speculation and mythology, *ocean* means the still, vast abyss of Being, as in the familiar analogy of our lives being a drop of water in the great ocean of Brahma.

Philosophical generalization, therefore, will continue to be a primary source of intercultural and interreligious understanding. Our thinking, in both the Judeo-Christian-Islamic West and the Hindu-Buddhist-Confucian East will always be argument in some sense. The question is whether Christians can hold to the belief that Jesus Christ is Lord of the human community without exercising the aggressive logic of persuasion and control in defense of that belief.

But if the intent of one's argument is not to persuade, then what might it be? Here the old Protestant evangelical tradition of "testimony" or "witness" takes on new meaning. The original intent of that practice was not to prove that one was right and the other wrong. It was a liturgical celebration of one's religious affections and an offering of one's religious insight. While the idea of "winning souls for Christ" eventually made this practice aggressive and controlling, at its best it was not an attempt to get something; it was an attempt to give something.

This is not to embrace that increasingly popular relativism in which people of differing faiths are urged to present their beliefs to one another with the diffident preface, "This is only what I happen to believe." Such a weak claim trivializes both the believer and the belief. The only religious faith worth serious attention is a passionate conviction; but there is a substantial difference between the celebration of passionate conviction and the manipulative exercise of passionate persuasion so characteristic of contemporary American televangelism and the telemarketing techniques it employs.

The exclusivistic logic that rationally requires persuasion may well be appropriate to a situation in which we know for certain the outcome of an action or a belief. We persuade little children not to touch a hot stove, for example, because we know for certain that they will hurt themselves if they do. Within some areas of experience our knowledge is predictive and conclusive in this way. To know causes is to predict effects. Technical reason is generally predictive and conclusive in this way, and the principle of noncontradiction is everywhere affirmed in these areas of experience.

But our knowledge in regard to fundamental human ventures such as work and love is no longer immediately predictive or entirely conclusive. The logic of mature experience is increasingly experimental, or, if you will, dialectical. Today's best guess yields to tomorrow's antithesis, and the concluding synthesis is but a new thesis that awaits its inevitable antithesis. It was because he understood this dialectical nature of experience that Hegel flirted with a rejection of the principle of noncontradiction.

Wise parents who no longer seek to control their grown children with conclusive arguments are not weakening in their own beliefs; they are recognizing that their understanding of their children's lives is no longer predictive and conclusive. Conversation then becomes an exploratory appeal to the other's beliefs and experience. This openness to the other is one of the fruits of love, but its substance is the mystery of human experience, particularly the experience of the transcendent. At this level of experience and belief, the principle of non-contradiction becomes secondary to the paradoxes of love and faith.

A nonaggressive, enabling argument is primarily an appeal to the experience and beliefs of the other person. Like a work of art, it offers itself as a window on the world, not as a command to think in a specific way. It says, "This is my experience. Is it yours also? Does it have something of our common human experience in it?" We are so accustomed to argument as an attack concluding with a logical closure that anything else seems initially soft-headed. The result, however, is that some crucially important arguments have been vitiated by trying to meet the conclusive/exclusive demands of technical reason.

The curious history of the ontological argument for the existence of God is a case in point. Very few modern philosophers have accepted the argument as valid technical proof for the existence of God.[3] It was regarded widely as having only that philosophical significance which attaches to grandiose failures. Having been decisively refuted by Kant, it nevertheless continued to resurface in philosophical dialogue. The reason for this surprising recurrence is that the argument describes the way believers reflect philosophically on the reality of God. The argument does not prove that God exists; it only outlines the rational structure of belief in God. It proves that belief in God is not irrational, and that the reality of God is an appropriate subject for philosophical reflection.

Argument as appeal does not forsake the principle of non-contradiction in clarifying particular ideas, but because fundamental ideas are always open-ended appeals to each person's experience and belief, the context of one's ideas is the coherence of lived experience. Since the ontological coherence of experience transcends the technical principle of noncontradiction, philosophers like Marcel have argued against structuring a philosophical point of view as a system under the constraints of technical reason.[4] His point was that a philosophy ought to be structured more like a life than like a machine. Marcel's work is a continuing experiment with Christian philosophy as enabling rather than persuading, appealing rather than proving. He initially presented his philosophy as a metaphysical journal in order to make that point. That book was dedicated to his philosophical mentors, Henri Bergson and William Ernest Hocking, both of whom presented their philosophies in a comparably open-ended spirit and form as philosophies of life.

If the Christian faith is to be "good news" to a postmodern world, its concern for a peaceful human community must come as a gift, and an appeal, not as coercive rationale. Perhaps the most effective form of Christian contribution to interreligious intercultural dialogue will be a rethinking of ideas about God, Christ, the church, and the Kingdom in this new context. This requires more than simply retelling the Christian story. It involves the use of philosophical notions and constructs to articulate the meaning of the Christian faith in our new historical period. And, as with the second function of philosophy in the life of the early church, it will involve critical distinctions among various interpretations of Christian truth within the Christian tradition. The spirit of tribalism is still strong in certain areas of Christian life and thought and must be fought. But the third function of philosophy in the life of the early church must be transformed into an instrument of enablement. The question is not who has the best religion. The question is what is the best each religion has to offer to the human community. How, then, might we begin to rethink ideas of God, Christ, the church and the Kingdom?

When ideas of God are formulated in various sacred writings, they range from the "nothingness" of some Buddhist schools to the "cosmic person" of some Christian schools. Because Christianity is a "religion of the book," like Judaism

and Islam, its understanding of God is centered in the revelation that is set forth in its sacred book or scripture. The
emphasis in Christian scripture is that God is the God of Israel
and the God and Father of Jesus Christ. There are intimations
in the Old Testament that God is the God of peoples other
than Israel, but this idea is never developed fully. In the New
Testament there are hints that God can be known on the basis
of human experience apart from revelation, as Paul suggests
in the first chapter of his letter to the church at Rome, but
this affirmation is negligible compared to the significance of
God's revelation in the event of Christ's resurrection.

In the history of the church, however, there has been a
tradition of natural or philosophical theology that has taken
its point of departure from rational reflection on human experience, rather than the revelation of scripture. From Saint
Thomas to Tillich it has been argued that this natural or
philosophical knowledge of God is real but incomplete. The
fullness of who God is can be known only through the revelation, but that there is a God is knowable through reason
and experience. Because Christian thought is responsible to
the church for articulating and defending the fullness of Christian faith, natural theology has been a secondary tradition.
However, if there is to be a world civil religion in which a
planetary people can find a religious dimension for understanding the nature of human community, this common
ground for reflection on a natural theology becomes more
significant.

H. Richard Niebuhr called this venture Christian philosophy, and that is my understanding of my own work.[5] It is
Christian insofar as its reflection takes place against the background of the biblical revelation of God, even though it does
not call directly on that revelation as a source of authority or
attempt to do justice to the fullness of that revelation. It is
philosophy insofar as it engages the common philosophical
task of reflecting rationally on the nature of human experience, as Marxist, Buddhist, and Hindu philosophies do. It will
not be what has recently been thought of as philosophy of

religion, since that discipline is an objective philosophical evaluation of ideas from various religious traditions. A Christian philosophy focuses on the Christian understanding of human experience, as a Marxist philosophy does with Marxism, or a Hindu philosophy does with Hinduism.

A Christian philosophy cannot expect to find very much common ground with philosophers of other traditions concerning the nature of God. In fact, it does not need very much common ground. Elements of agreement on a common human view of God need only be vague and minimal in order to serve the needs of the civil religion essential to a human community. The methods of this exploration will be largely phenomenological. It is not possible to invent a common human perception of God if the elements of such a view are not already present and functioning.

Part of this rethinking must necessarily involve those present criticisms of the Christian idea of God which have already been proposed by those who have identified themselves as oppressed. To what extent are liberation theologians right when they accuse North American and European theologians of bourgeois values in suppressing the revolutionary commandments of the biblical God?

Is the notion of praxis an appropriate substitute for the methods of abstraction and generalization that Christian theology has inherited from Greek philosophy and that have characterized Christian definitions of God?[6]

To what extent are black theologians right in arguing that the Christian church has been dominated by white racism, thereby vitiating its claim to embody a new inclusive human community in Christ?[7]

Are feminists right in arguing that a patriarchal society has produced a doctrine of God that is sexually exclusivistic?[8]

These concerns are part of the agenda for a Christian philosophy that comes from within the Christian tradition. From outside Christianity the compelling question about God centers on God's relation to human history and the sense in which God is or is not metaphysically distinguishable from the human soul. Here the question must be asked whether the notion of God in the religions of the book in the West is different enough from notions of the transcendent in the great religions of the East so that a new language may be needed in order to make conversation possible.

Such a language will need to be based on the way in which the people of various religious cultures actually speak of the transcendent, and not on academic comparisons of intellectual traditions. The purpose of reconstructing an idea of God is not primarily to bring intellectual coherence to various views, but to find the common ground that is actually there in the living faith of various believers. From the Christian side the motivation for such an exploration is the conviction that God is a presence for us all in history, not just a transcendental idea; that the *imago dei* is the fundamental nature of human-kind; and that God is at work in history to make a peaceable Kingdom a reality, calling us to join in that work.

Ideas of God exist on three major levels. One is "folk religion," or "village" religion, the actual belief structure of people as various as tribal Africans, South Asian villagers, native American tribes, and rural people in the mountains of Tennessee, the highlands of Scotland, and the plains of Siberia and northern China. In the common, natural religion of such folk, God is a powerful and brooding presence, determining seed time and harvest, giving new birth and taking away the dying. God is often only another name for what philosophers call fate, but the fact that such folk are religious in their understanding of fate witnesses to humankind's instinct for the transcendent.

The second level is that of the great world religions, and here there is considerable diversity in the understanding of God. It is significant, however, that there is overlap among religious cultures. Christian Unitarians have more in common with Hindus of the Ramakrishna Mission than they have with fundamentalist Protestant or Roman Catholic Christians, for example.

The third level is that of mystical experience and the "perennial philosophy," grounded in Neoplatonism, that structures its world view. As with folk religion, there are strong common characteristics in the mysticism of all religious traditions. While mystical theology is necessarily a "negative theology," presenting a view of God in terms of what God is not, there is common positive content in the mystic's experience of the *mysterium tremendum* and its compelling power to command attention (*fascinans*).[9] The phenomenology of religion would therefore seem to show a common human experience of a transcendent reality that at least compels human attention and is believed to determine human destiny. It is this dimension of transcendence in human experience that civil religion draws on in making loyalty to a political community something more profound than mere nationalism or patriotism. It is a human reality that elicits loyalty to the human community. Reflection on a natural theology of God thus reveals some common experiential grounding for an integrated idea of human community.

A fully developed Christian idea of God, however, is inseparable from an understanding of Jesus, the Christ. From within the Christian tradition the recurring quest of the historical Jesus has raised fundamental questions about the nature of faith and the relation between the church's faith in its risen Lord and the historic facts—if such there be—of Jesus' life and death and resurrection.[10] From outside the Christian tradition, however, a compelling question has gone largely unanswered. The question is: Why do you say that Jesus is somehow God?

The question is not asked unsympathetically. Because of the worldwide spread of Christianity, Jesus' story is widely known and he is admired and even loved by many who are not Christians. At the council of Chalcedon in the fourth century, Catholic Christianity formulated the doctrine of the two natures of Christ: one human, one divine. This formulation was based on a notion of substance taken from the

ancient Greek philosophy that still informed Christian
thought. However, with the rise of modern philosophy, dominated by notions of nature taken from Darwinian biology
and Newtonian physics, ideas of substance were gradually
superseded by ideas of process. To many who are not Christian but who are nevertheless captivated by the story of Jesus,
Christian affirmations of Christ's divinity remain obscurantist, both religiously and intellectually.

Is there an open-ended interpretation of Jesus' experience
that can at least make sense of the affirmation that Jesus the
Christ is both fully human and distinctively divine? An earlier
evangelical theology was so aggressive in preaching the lordship of Jesus Christ over all the world that it ignored the
inherent incomprehensibility of its own affirmation. The fundamental paradox of the Incarnation cannot finally be resolved into a seamless, systematic rationale. But Christian
thought must be reasonably clear about the divinity of Jesus.
Such an explanation will not have the tight coherence of technical reason, but it can have the ontological coherence of lived
experience.

The religious importance of the doctrine of incarnation
was that it made specific the *mysterium tremendum* of human
experience. This God is not just the mystery brooding over
all things. God is personal presence, with us and for us. God
is our God, and we are God's people. This is not a God afar
off, but a God who "comes down" to be with us. And this
"being with" is no metaphor or abstract quality of the divine.
This *Gott mit uns* becomes one with us, becomes a person
who shares our history with us. God is our friend and
neighbor.[11]

So the idea of incarnation grounds the notion of community in the reality of God. Our relation to God is not
primarily an identity discovered inwardly. It is primarily a
relationship discovered with another person, this Jesus who
is God with us. Hence the Christian idea of devotion to God
is not primarily "spiritual," since to love God is to love the

neighbor. It is primarily relational or communal. To love God is to make human community.

There are two sides to classical Christian affirmations about the divinity of Jesus. One is the Logos christology of John's gospel, which affirms that Christ was the Word of God in the beginning. The other is that Jesus, as a fully human person in history, *became* divine in the course of his human life, through "adoption" into God. This adoptionist christology must explain how this divine power could have been part of the life of the historical Jesus, and how that event came about.[12]

Augustine's doctrine of the soul is a helpful point of departure for such an explanation. It focuses on the will as the seat of the human spirit. Rudolf Bultmann's study *Primitive Christianity* points out that this emphasis marked a clear distinction between emergent Christian thought and the philosophical presuppositions of Hellenism.[13] Hellenism viewed human nature as grounded in the mind; hence the human problem was essentially one of understanding, and religious salvation resulted from a kind of knowledge.

For Christian thought, the Old Testament emphasis on obedience to God as the mark of faithfulness is modified but remains intact. This becomes apparent when reflecting on the difficulty of defining *faith* as a noun in New Testament writings. The notion becomes clear only when one asks what it means to be faithful, and faith becomes an adjective or an adverb. The New Testament abounds with illustrations of faithfulness to the living God. To be faithful is to do what the Samaritan did, what the father of the prodigal son did, and so forth. Christ's divinity, therefore, concerns the relation of his will to the will of God, especially the idea of *kenosis* or self-emptying of Christ's will.

This tradition emphasizes the self-emptying of Christ's spirit in order to be filled with the spirit of God. Jesus' prayer in the Garden of Gethsemane asks that "this cup might pass" from him but he nevertheless seeks to do "the

Father's will," and not his own.[14]

This self-emptying of one's will is both difficult and dangerous. Personality integration is not instinctive and automatic as with physical integrations like breathing. The body breathes and circulates its blood by itself, without mental effort, whereas psychic integration is maintained by a subtle, pervasive, and constant act of will. Even in extreme cases of functional disability such as catatonic schizophrenia, there is still an element of will maintaining a subsistence level of psychic function. The failure of this minimal subsistence will-to-live is perhaps most evident in the seriously ill, some of whom recover, and others of whom, even given the same prognosis, do not. It is common lore among doctors that in order for patients to recover from a serious illness they have to want to get better.

The case of the seriously ill patient who "gives up" is a clue to a different phenomenon: the seriously faithful religious person who "gives over." Sacrificial love always involves giving over part of one's life—one's interest, one's need, one's desire—for the well-being of the other. But sacrificial love is not uncommon. Within the bonds of family life, especially in the constant care of mothers for children, sacrificial love becomes one of the common graces of human experience. A less common and more dramatic example of sacrificial love is found in ethical heroism, where martyrs die for their beliefs, or soldiers sacrifice their own lives for their comrades.

In each of these instances, however, the sacrificial act is a fulfillment of one's own life. Sacrifice is a conscious closure to the meaning of being oneself. If one could be privy to the innermost thoughts of a person in the midst of a sacrificial act, I suspect we would discover a small element of self-observing awareness. The soldier who throws himself on a grenade to save his buddies is probably faintly mindful of being a good soldier.

In any event, such acts of sacrificial love are all relational. It is specific love for another human being, for our own kind, and—within families—for our own flesh and blood. To sacrifice oneself for an ideological cause is to identify the meaning of one's own life with the life of the cause. But here one is still within the realm of human life-meanings, and they are tangible and comprehensible. They are not fraught with the demonic mystery of the transcendental *mysterium tremendum et fascinans* of God.

To give oneself over to God is to suffer the whirlwind. In psychological terms it is to go crazy. To let your life run out into God is to let go of the integrating function of the will which holds the psychic self together. It is to suffer disintegration. It is psychic death. It risks disintegration in the faithful hope that God will reintegrate one's life in terms of God's will, and not one's own. One gives one's life to God for God to make it his own.

In the story of Jesus' faithfulness to God this possibility becomes a reality. The divinizing of Christ, his "adoption" by God, is his willingness to suffer psychic disintegration and the mystery of his reintegration by God's spirit. This event is the substance of the claim that "truly this man was the Son of God." This view does not necessarily require exclusivistic metaphysical claims that this self-giving is unrepeatable. That claim is part of Logos christology's presuppositions. It only notes that, as far as most of us know, this event has no exact religious parallel.

And against those Christians who suggest that Jesus' faithfulness is a role model for us all, it notes only that our regularly experienced acts of self-sacrifice are modest, minimal, and finally self-protective. We guard ourselves very carefully against going crazy. We are glad to be ethical and self-sacrificial within limits. Limitless self-sacrifice; self-sacrifice without prior assurance; suffering the whirlwind; we regularly stop short of all this. And it is precisely because we stop short that the example of Jesus, who did not stop short, is no model for what we should do. It is something more important than that.

He is one who crossed over into God, and whose person and work therefore have a special authority for us. He is an authoritative word of the God who has become a participant with us in the tribulations of human experience, and through whose life and death and resurrection we have come to know who God is.

The distinctiveness of the Christian faith centers in its understanding of God. Through the trinitarian doctrine of God as Incarnate Lord, God becomes a concrete historic reality in our world in the person and work of Jesus, the Christ. The Christian notion of the church as the body of Christ is therefore an inseparable part of the notion of God as Father-Son-Spirit, Creator, Incarnate Lord, and Redeemer. The idea of the church as the body of Christ is the characteristic Christian way of saying that God is not only transcendently beyond us, but also immanently with us. The function of sacrament in Christian life makes that religious idea tangible in the communion elements of bread and wine, the staples of life; it makes it ethical in the promises of baptism, confirmation, and marriage; and above all it makes it communal in binding us to God and to one another in a historic community whose work and worship is the power and presence of the God who is actually with us.

The aspect of human experience to which the Christian faith does special justice, therefore, is the problem of loneliness; not primarily as a psychological or sociological phenomenon, but as metaphysical alienation from oneself, one's fellows, and whatever reality lies at the ultimate heart of things. The Christian faith is good news to any who have known themselves, in this sense, to be lost. The good news is that we have a home, not just in the end, and not just as spiritual reality or as the result of an esoteric metaphysical insight, but tangibly, concretely, historically, here and now. That home is the actual historic community we share with our neighbors and with God.

The actual historic church, however, has been corrupted by sectarianism, exclusivism, and triumphalism. A community which originally opened out to a new humanity readily became another institution in a world of institutions. That institutionalization was necessary in order for the church to be a historically redemptive community. What was also necessary, however, was an awareness that the church as institution was only one form of a larger historic reality in which the institution participated, and which gave the institution its grounding. That larger reality is the community of Christ's body, which is identified not by institutional affiliation but by faithfulness to the continuing movement of the Spirit.

Paul had announced that to be "in Christ" was to live the reality of love. And Jesus' parable of the Kingdom in Matthew's gospel made it clear that those who were the community of his ongoing life were those who did the will of the Father in feeding the hungry, clothing the naked, and caring for those whom the world had abandoned.

There is much discussion in current Christian thought, both Catholic and Protestant, about the status of "anonymous Christians," the "invisible church," and other ideas that might indicate the wideness of God's redemptive mercy and the fact that much of the work of the Kingdom is done by those who are not Christians.[15] Many of these reflections are vitiated, however, by taking the institutional church as the point of departure for their reflection.

The ecclesiastical institution is a limited expression of the more inclusive body of Christ. The church became an institution, but it was originally, and remains essentially, a movement. It is a "gathering" of people faithful to God. In order to counter the alienating forces of triumphalism and exclusivism that have bedeviled the history of the church, this wider understanding of the body of Christ is a more creative point of departure for thinking about the church. Various movements in social, political, and cultural life, including non-Christian religious groups, participate in this historic "body." The new ecumenical adventure is rediscovering the meaning of Jesus' affirmation that many will come "from East and West and North and South" to sit at table together in the Kingdom; people who are not Christians, but who serve God and participate in the more inclusive body of Christ.[16]

The Kingdom of God is both the purpose of our present history and the eschatological reality that remains when history is completed. To speak of the Kingdom is to raise the question of eternal life in response to the basic human question, What happens to us when we die?

The most developed doctrine of eternal life in contemporary Christian thought is in Paul Tillich's *Systematic Theology*, and the irony of his doctrine is that it is not clearly contrary to a naturalistic conception of death.[17] Through an existentialist understanding of time—whereby both past and future are collapsed into the present, on the grounds that the present is the only actual moment that is immediately real—Tillich can speak persuasively and profoundly about eternity as a dimension of each present moment, without, however, confronting the traditional question about what happens when we die.

A prospective danger of this question is that it could raise again the old triumphalist exclusivism of Christian ecclesiology, and its medieval doctrines of heaven, hell, and purgatory. The present danger, however, is that a question of considerable seriousness may simply be ignored. If it makes no ultimate difference to my destiny as a person whether I cared for the world's abandoned or not, then a Stoic ethic of doing in this life what I choose to call good simply because it gives meaning to my life makes sense; but the Christian affirmation does not. It is one thing to bemoan those times when the hope of heaven and the fear of hell were primary motivating forces for Christian ethics; it is something else to think that we can do without a Christian notion of life after death.

The Hindu philosophy of salvation and the "peace which passes all understanding" is probably the most widely held current belief about the afterlife. The problem of the Hindu doctrine of *moksa* and the ultimate unity of my inner soul or *atman* and the Holy World Power of *Brahman* is that the Hindu doctrine of salvation is also difficult to distinguish from a naturalistic concept of death.

There is great power in this idea, especially in *Advaita Vedanta*,[18] that the religious secret is simply the secret of the life process; that the one thing we all most yearn for is not to have to worry or care or hurt anymore; and that this is the one thing that life promises absolutely, because at the end there is nothing. In this view death is not the Great Enemy; death is finally the Great Deliverer.

Is there hope for a far country? Or is our best hope only that the pain of life in the near country will not follow us beyond the grave? Is there continuity to our purposes? Or does religious humility mean that our human purposes appropriately end with human life?

And are the people we care about still there, someplace, in a world beyond our world, or a world within our world, where it is possible to be in touch with them, not only today, but tomorrow and tomorrow and tomorrow? Or is that only the child in us, crying out for an assurance that is no longer anyone's to give?

Perhaps it is here that Christian thought has been most audacious. Simple surcease from pain is not the peace sought by the people of the cross. Part of the Christian affirmation is that we must not fail our heart's desire; that only to want out is not to want enough; that the God who calls and cares for us saves us in a manner beyond our farthest imagining.

Postscript

Claiming a New Identity in the Human Tribe

BLOOD is the primal bond in a traditional society, and blood is the necessary binding ingredient for a planetary human community. We cannot escape nuclear holocaust with only liberal prudential plans for economic justice or conservative ideological persuasions about the virtues of democracy. We will be saved from the ultimate horror of self-destruction only by a vague, visceral identification of the other as somehow one with us, part of a family that we must preserve at all costs. "This fragile earth, our island home," depends for its future on our claiming a new identity, no longer racial, or regional, not linguistic or one of class and caste, not even religious, but one that claims our common humanity as primary blood bond.

Blood identity, of course, has always been a myth. One of modern science's gifts to philosophical anthropology is the realization that blood is empirically distinguishable only by universal types. Our race has nothing to do with our empirical blood. But that little bit of technological reasoning helps not at all in understanding why blood has been such a powerful natural bond. What it has really meant, we can now see, is our fundamental human need for participation in an intimate community, a family.

And why do we cling so fiercely to this primal bond? Because we, as individuals, need assurance about our place in the maelstrom of our world. Otherwise we are lost. We need to know where we belong. "Home," said Robert Frost, "is where, when you have to go there, they have to take you in." Blood is a symbol for human intimacy. It is with our blood community, our "kin-folk," that we feel most at home.

And this intimacy, we must confess, does need some confirming sense that we are who we are because we stand over against those others. In these intimate matters of identity, there can be no strong sense of *us*, unless there is some sense that we belong to a specific, intimate community set over against some group or entity or realm that is somehow different from us. For this reason, no gift of modern science to philosophical anthropology is greater than the technological achievement of placing a human person on the moon.

At that moment, one of us turned and looked back at planet Earth. It was cold, and blue, and beautiful, and home. For the first time in the history of our human race, home had become the planet as such. With that "one small step for a man," a planetary consciousness was born. Now, for the first time, it is no longer simply sentimental to speak of the human family, or to think of humankind as the blood connection that binds all sorts and conditions of human folk together. For we saw ourselves as an island people, perhaps lost in the stars, but nevertheless over against a vast void of no known habitation. Contemporary astronomers construct elaborate systems for messages to the cosmos, regularly pooh-poohing the naive notion that, in an order so vast and complex, ours should be the only intelligent life. In the meantime, the rest of us note only that, thus far, there have been no replies.

Darkness and void without. And, within our island home, the will to hurt everywhere set loose.

Elie Wiesel's stories bear witness to the incomprehensible horror of the Nazi holocaust. We want to put that outburst of genocide behind us. We want to think of it as an aberration

of Hitler's Germany, but the killing fields of Cambodia and
Uganda and Indonesia have made genocide a continuing fact
of our history. The incomprehensible horror goes on and on.
And the worst may be yet to come. Nuclear holocaust, then
nuclear winter.

> Fire, then ice;
> Cosmic darkness;
> The void brought home;
> And no stories left to tell.

Ernest Hocking acknowledged this threat but saw the beginnings of a common human identity in a peculiar feature
of modern individualism. The individual claims his or her
right, mindful that he or she is claiming that same right for
others also. This is the difference between a right and an
interest. I am always alone in claiming *my* interest; but to
claim my *right* is to claim the rights of all others similarly
placed, and therefore to be in community with them.

This bond with one another, increasingly recognized, initiates a tribal sense of human community. The citizenry of
democratic societies have come to take their rights for granted,
as a natural given, like the ontological status of being a Tamil
in traditional Indian society. This "givenness" is paradoxically
strengthened by genocide, the very event that most threatens
it. Genocide elicits horror and despair, but the horror expresses an unshakable conviction that this is wrong; that all
people, as human beings, have a right to live.

Like the given beliefs of a traditional society, this sense
of one's right and one's bond with others is both vague and
visceral. We cannot prove it; we are not sure quite where it
came from. We are no less certain of it, however, for all that.
And as that certainty grows among us, our conviction that
we are part of a human family grows with it.

On one level at least, the human community is shaping
its own tribal blood identity. Some Christians will insist on
claiming this view of human rights as a Christian doctrine.

They will note that John Locke, in support of the most influential eighteenth-century statement of rights based on natural law, appealed to Hooker's *Laws of Ecclesiastical Polity*, and that the influential American Declaration of Independence drew heavily on Christian ideas and values.

This claim is overstated, however, and it misses the point. It is overstated because there are numerous influences at work in modern notions of human rights. Various religious and secular traditions have contributed to it. It misses the point because the relevant question is no longer "To whom does this idea belong?" but "To whom can this idea be of service?" If Christians have made a contribution—and they have—let them rejoice in that service. But let them also be humbled by the fact that, as long as it was simply and solely Christian, the idea of human rights could not serve the world. Only when it was given away as part of civil religion could it become an established belief in the larger human community.

In their institutional, ecclesiastical life the great world religions are still essentially tribal communities. When they are willing to "lose their life," however, and give over what is best in them to the commonweal, they participate in that civil religion that embodies our convictions about human rights, deepens our commitment to the human tribe, and gives us hope for peace and a human future.

Notes

Introduction

1. See Carl Friedrich, "Pan-Humanism, Culturism, and the Federal Union of Europe," in *Philosophy, Religion, and the Coming World Civilization*, ed. Leroy S. Rouner (The Hague: Martinus Nijhoff, 1966), pp. 330–39.

2. Josiah Royce, *The Philosophy of Loyalty* (New York: Macmillan, 1913), and *The Hope of the Great Community* (New York: Macmillan, 1916).

3. My experience of Timmy's death is the subject of *The Long Way Home* (South Bend, Ind.: Langford Books, 1989).

1. Christianity and Tribalism

1. Josh. 24:2. All references are to the Revised Standard Version. With regard to tribal blood unity, see Exod. 24:8 where Moses, throwing blood from sacrificed animals upon the book of the covenant, calls this "the blood of the covenant which the Lord made with you." Vis-à-vis the danger and persistence of old religious practices that Moses encounters, see Exod. 34:11–28. For the evolution of a sacred figure in various mythologies, see Emile Durkheim, *The Elementary Forms of the Religious Life*, trans. Joseph Ward Swain (Glencoe, Ill.: Free Press, 1958), esp. his presentation of "elementary religion" in Australian totemic cults.

On the dangers of retribalization, see George E. Mendenhall's essay, "Biblical History in Transition," in *The Bible and the Ancient Near East: Essays in Honor of William Foxwell Albright*, ed. G. Ernest Wright (Garden City, N.Y.: Doubleday, 1961). See esp. p. 44: "[The] covenant bond gradually gave way to a commonly accepted view that it was a blood tie which held the people together, since the religion became less effective as an actual unifying factor."

2. Gen. 13:16.

3. See Gen. 11:1–10. *Babel* is the Hebrew name for Babylon. *Babil* in Assyrian means "gate of god." Some etymologies draw a parallel between *babil* and the Hebrew verb *balal* ("to confuse") in Gen. 11:9. See Charles Laymon, *The Interpreter's One-Volume Commentary on the Bible* (New York: Abingdon Press, 1971), pp. 9–10.

The original Fall of humanity was occasioned by the choice, not of the tree of life, but of the fruit of the tree of knowledge of good and evil (cf. parallels in Hellenic cults and philosophers of Greek language in C. M. Dodd, *The Bible and the Greeks* [London: Hoder and Stoughton, 1935], pt. 2, chap. 7, "Hellenistic Judaism and the Hermetica"), a knowledge which would have lifted humans to the position of God. There are two parallel orders of unity in the Babel narrative. The first is the unity of language—or social cohesion—posited directly by the myth. The second is the symbol of the tower, which human beings construct and which becomes the expression of the unification of humankind and God by means of knowledge. Roman Jakobson analyzes the magico-religious function of language both as socially integrative and as metaphoric in so far as a tower embodies the unity personified as a being. See Jakobson's article in *Style in Language*, ed. Thomas Sebeok (Cambridge, Mass.: MIT Press, 1960), pp. 350–77. Discussion of the magico-religious function of language is in "Minutes of the Study Group in Linguistics and Psycho-analysis" (New Psychoanalytical Institute, New York, 1964, typescript).

4. Deut. 24:17–18.

5. Frederick C. Grant, *Hellenistic Religions: The Age of Synchretism* (New York: Liberal Arts Press, 1953), "Introduction," pp. xv ff.; John Herman Randall, Jr., *Hellenistic Ways of Deliverance and the Making of the Christian Synthesis* (New York: Columbia University Press, 1970), esp. chap. 9, "The Making of the Christian Synthesis," chap. 10, "The Gospel of John and the Mystery Cult of Paul," and chap. 12, "The Christian Philosophy of the Greek Fathers," pp. 135–44, 145–58, 165–83.

6. From the time of Abraham, circumcision was the ultimate sign of the Hebrews' alliance with God, to whom in Gen. 17:10–14 God gives the command: "You shall be circumcised in the flesh of your foreskins and it shall be a sign of the covenant between me

and you." Hence circumcision served the dual function of ritual purification necessary to the establishment of a household and as a blood offering to God as sign of the alliance. For anthropological analyses of the originality of the Hebrew use of circumcision, see Noureddine Toualbi, *La Circoncision: Blessure narcissique ou promotion sociale* (Algiers: Société national d'édition et de diffusion, 1975); see also Bruno Bettelheim's remarks on circumcision and Judaism in his *Symbolic Wounds: Puberty Rites and the Envious Male* (Glencoe, Ill.: Free Press, 1954).

Paul, however, states, "He is not a real Jew who is one outwardly, nor is true circumcision something external . . . real circumcision is a matter of the heart, spiritual not literal" (Rom. 2:28–29). See also Rom. 4:10 and 1 Cor. 7:18. Gal. 5:6 and 6:15, Eph. 2:11–12, Col. 2:11, and Col. 3:11 all place faith above outward signs of election.

7. See Lev. 26:41 and Ezek. 44:7–9.

8. See Matt. 12:1–5, 10–13; Mark 2:23–27 and 3:1–6; and Luke 6:1–5.

9. See Dietrich Bonhoeffer, *Christ the Center*, trans. John Bowden (New York: Harper and Row, 1966), pp. 47 ff.; esp. pt. 1, "The Present Christ: The Pro-me," pp. 47–63.

2. The Christian Affirmation

1. On Jesus' understanding of the Kingdom of God, see Mark 1:15; Matt. 4:17, 10:17, and 12:28, where Jesus speaks of the Kingdom being "at hand." The vision of the Kingdom is illustrated by the parable of the mustard seed (Matt. 13:31–32; Mark 4:30–32; Luke 13:20–21), the parable of the yeast (Matt. 13:33; Luke 13:20–21), and the parable of the great feast (Matt. 22:1–10; Luke 14:15–24). See also the passages in John concerning spiritual rebirth and the Kingdom of Heaven; John 3:3–6 and 18:36.

2. Note in this regard Karl Jaspers's figurative identification of the Western individual with "the Christian" in his *Der philosophische Glaube angesichts der Offenbarung* (Munich: Piper Verlag, 1962), p. 52.

3. See Karl Rahner, *Foundations of Christian Faith: An Introduction to the Idea of Christ*, trans. William Van Dyck (New York:

Seabury Press, 1978), chap. 7, "Christianity as Church," sec. 5.2, pp. 348–59. In this work the church as "latent" and capable of self-actualization is discussed in light of questions of ecumenism and the necessity of a united church in and of Christ.

Rahner distinguishes the "visible versus invisible church" in chap. 13, "Spirituality," in *A Rahner Reader*, ed. Gerald A. McCool (New York: Seabury Press, 1975), pp. 322–29. The comments in this chapter are taken from Rahner's major work, *Theological Investigations: Further Theology of Spiritual Life*, vol. 8 (London: Darton, Longman, and Todd, 1971), pp. 159–67.

4. Rahner writes of God's use of anonymous believers toward the promotion of the "absolute future" in "The Christian Future of Man" and "The Church and the Parousia of Christ," in *A Rahner Reader*, pp. 343–47 and 348–51. Here the church is described as "the community of those who already possess the eschatological gift which is God himself, who in full liberty really accept this possession" (p. 348). See also Paul Tillich, *Systematic Theology*, 3 vols. (New York and Evanston, Ill.: University of Chicago Press, 1951–67), vol. 2, chap. 2, "The Spiritual Presence," pp. 153 ff.

5. See Isa. 45:1 –7.

6. See n. 1 above; further, see Pss. 103:19, 145:11–13, and, with reference to the ideal of Kingdom as "a life to come out of death," see Dan. 12:1–14 and Isa. 32:18–20, 66:6–14. The allusion to the Kingdom as a "new age" is found in Isa. 32:15–20.

7. See Rudolf Bultmann, *Theology of the New Testament*, trans. Kendrick Grobel, 2 vols. (New York: Charles Scribner's Sons, 1955), 1:37–42, 47–52, on the forms of "eschatological consciousness" within the early congregation. See also Reinhold Niebuhr, *The Nature and Destiny of Man: A Christian Interpretation*, vol. 2, *Human Destiny* (London: Nisbet, 1943), chap. 2, "The Disclosure and the Fulfillment of the Meaning of Law and History," pp. 36–70. Finally, see Jürgen Moltmann, *Theology of Hope: On the Ground and the Implications of a Christian Eschatology* (New York: Harper and Row, 1967), chap. 3, "The Resurrection and Future of Jesus Christ," esp. secs. 12 and 13, "The Future of Life" and "The Future of the Kingdom of God," pp. 208–24.

8. For a discussion of love as the "essence" of Christianity and the "content" of its ethical demand, see Bultmann, *Theology of the*

New Testament, 2:222. See also Reinhold Niebuhr's presentation of the relation of justice to love in Christian ethics in *The Nature and Destiny of Man*, 2:255 ff.

3. The Christian Problem

1. I am relying heavily here upon Peter Brown's biography of Augustine, *Augustine of Hippo: A Biography* (Berkeley and Los Angeles: University of California Press, 1969).

2. Ibid., chap. 27, "Civitas Peregrina," pp. 316 ff. The contemporary echoes of this "project" show the significance and power of its formulation in Augustine. When Karl Barth remarked that "God speaks to me through the Bible and through the newspaper," he spoke, as Pierre-Jean Labarrière put it, to the "mission" of Christianity in the world and in history, such that Christianity "constitutes in each age and each cultural milieu a sort of reservoir of symbolization [réserve de symbolisation] which, of itself, unfolds in every area of human existence in order to find therein the body and contents of the truth which it carries. . . . In this way, the believer, in the very act wherein he confesses that Christ is truth, recognizes that this truth comes to him not only through the channel of Scripture and the sacraments, but through the entire content of religious and secular existence in which he [the believer] finds himself engaged" (Pierre-Jean Labarrière, *Dieu Aujourd'hui: Cheminement rationnel, décision de liberté* [Paris: Desclée, 1977], p. 215 [trans. Bettina Bergo]).

3. Brown, *Augustine of Hippo*, chap. 16, "The Confessions," pp. 158–81. Note esp. pp. 167–71 where the *Confessions* are seen as an exploration of the philosopher-theologian's will.

4. Rom. 7:19.

5. Brown, *Augustine of Hippo*, p. 319. For a discussion of Augustine's arguments for an archetypal interpretation of the Cain and Abel narrative, see pp. 320 ff. See also Étienne Gilson, *L'esprit de la philosophie médiévale*, 2d ed. (Paris: Librairie J. Vrin, 1983), esp. "La Providence chrétienne," pp. 158–60.

6. Note, with regard to the relationship between the Christian church as self-containing culture, as potential world culture, and as instrument for the proclamation of the gospel, Dietrich Bonhoeffer,

Ethics, trans. Eberhard Bethge (New York: Collier, 1955), chap. 7, pp. 291–302.

7. See Raimundo Panikkar, "La Sécularisation de l'herméneutique. Le cas du Christ: fils de l'homme et fils de Dieu," in *Herméneutique de la Sécularisation: Actes du Colloque organisé par le Centre international d'Études humanistes et de l'Institut d'Études philosophiques de Rome*, ed. Enrico Castelli (Paris: Aubier, Éditions Montaigne, 1976), pp. 213–18. Furthermore, secularization is conceived within Christian theologies—on the Catholic side, in the recent "political theologies" and "liberation theologies," and on the Protestant side, in the intuitions of Bonhoeffer on the "end of religion," in the theology of "secularization" of Harvey Cox, and in the "death of God" theology such as that of T.J.J. Altizer. For a discussion of this process of secularization, see French theologian Claude Geffré, "La Fonction idéologique de la sécularisation," in Castelli, ed., *Herméneutique de la Sécularisation*, pp. 112–40.

8. Paul Sevier Minear, *Eyes of Faith: A Study in the Biblical Point of View*, rev. ed. (St. Louis: Bethany Press, Abbott Books, 1966).

4. Modern Homelessness and the Individual

1. Discussions on the theme of metaphysical loneliness and modernity are too numerous to attempt to present comprehensively. Worthy of note are the following, which cover disciplines from philosophy through anthropology and narrative.

Jean-Jacques Rousseau discusses the theme of alienation and modernity versus the free development of the human person in his "Discourse on the Origin of Inequality" (e.g. the appended letter to Voltaire), in *The Social Contract and the Discourses* (New York: E. P. Dutton, 1913). Among more recent commentaries by philosophers is John Dewey, "The Individual in Cultural Crisis," in *Intelligence in the Modern World: John Dewey's Philosophy*, ed. Joseph Ratner (New York: Random House, 1939). French anthropologist and philosopher Louis Dumont has examined individualism from the point of view of contemporary anthropology in his *Essays on Individualism: Modern Ideology in Anthropological Perspective* (Chicago and London: University of Chicago Press, 1986). See also Claude Lefort on mutations in the concept of the political and the public sphere in his *Democracy and Political Theory*, trans. David Macey (Minneapolis: University of Minnesota Press, 1988). Of particular interest is Lefort's essay, "The Death of Immortality," in the above collection. For Lefort on the individual, bureaucracy, and totalitarian systems, see his *Political Forms of Modern Society: Bureaucracy, Democracy, and Totalitarianism*, ed. John B. Thompson (Cambridge, Mass.: MIT Press, 1986). In a narrative vein, see Camus's observations of American culture in his *American Journals*, trans. Hugh Levic (New York: Paragon, 1987), p. 43; and Simone de Beauvoir's journal, kept during her 1947 travels throughout the United States, *Amérique au jour le jour* (Paris: Éditions Paul Morihan, 1948). Sociologist Robert J. Lifton prolongs Simone de Beauvoir's type of analysis in *The Future of Immortality* (New York: Basic Books, 1987).

2. Quoted in Leroy S. Rouner, *Within Human Experience: The Philosophy of William Ernest Hocking* (Cambridge, Mass.: Harvard University Press, 1969), pp. 297 ff.

3. René Descartes, *Meditations on First Philosophy*. See Meditation 2 in *The Meditations and Selections from Principles of René Descartes*, trans. John Veitch (LaSalle, Ill.: Open Court Library of Philosophy, 1968), pp. 37 ff.

4. Immanuel Kant, *Critique of Pure Reason*, trans. Norman Kemp Smith (New York: MacMillan, 1965). Note the "Paralogisms of Pure Reason," pp. 332 ff. (A347, B405).

5. David Riesman, with Reuel Denny and Nathan Glazer, *The Lonely Crowd: A Study in Changing American Character* (New Haven: Yale University Press, 1966). See in particular pt. 1, "The Other-directed Round of Life," chaps. 6 and 7: "From Invisible Hand to Glad Hand," and "The Night Shift," pp. 130–47, 148–71. See also Robert Staughton Lynd, *Middletown: A Study in American Culture* (New York: Harcourt, Brace, 1956).

6. Thomas Hobbes, *Leviathan: Or the Matter, Forme, and Power of a Commonwealth Ecclesiastical and Civil* (London: Oxford University Press, 1967). For the discussion of all "motions in the head," the sensuous and the intellectual, see pt. 1, chap. 3, p. 19; and chap. 6, *passim*.

7. Ibid., chaps. 13–14, pp. 94–109.

8. Discussions of the impact of Einstein's relativity and of contemporary physics on the conceptions—both popular and philosophical—of the universe are numerous. See, for example, Alexander Koyré, *Newtonian Studies* (Chicago: University of Chicago Press, 1968). Also note the work of Ernst Cassirer, *Substance and Function and Einstein's Theory of Relativity* (New York: Dover, 1953), chaps. 6–7: "The Concept of Reality," pp. 271–308, and "Subjectivity and Objectivity of the Relational Concepts," pp. 309–25. Carl Friedrich von Weizäcker, *The World-view of Physics*, trans. Marjorie Green (Chicago: University of Chicago Press, 1952, examines relations between recent theories of physics and Kant's rationalist philosophy (chap. 4), the notion of our world (chap. 5), of natural laws (chap. 6), and of the relation obtaining between modern physics and the idea of the subject and object in experimental method (chap. 7). Finally, see the Czech philosopher of science Milič Čapek, *The Philosophical Impact of Contemporary Physics* (New York: Van Nostrand, Reinhold, 1961), in particular pt. 2, "The Disintegration of the Classical Framework and the Significance of New Concepts," pp. 143–381. And see Ilya Prigogine and Isabelle Stengers, *Order Out of Chaos: Man's New Dialogue with Nature* (New York: Bantam Books, 1984), esp. bk. 3, "From Being to Becoming."

5. Civil Religion and the American Dream

1. For the expectations and demise of the vision of the "melting pot" in the recent history of the city of New York, see Nathan Glazer and Daniel Patrick Moynihan, *Beyond the Melting Pot: The Negroes, Puerto Ricans, Jews, Italians, and Irish of New York City* (Cambridge, Mass.: MIT Press and Harvard University Press, 1963), "Introduction," pp. 1–23, and "Beyond the Melting Pot," pp. 288–315. See also Oscar Handlin, *The Uprooted: The Epic Story of the Great Migrations that Made the American People* (Boston: Little, Brown, 1951), for a discussion of the mechanism of failure within the melting pot concept in the America of the Gilded Age through the 1920s.

2. For an effective discussion of the New England renaissance prior to the Civil War, see Van Wyck Brooks's remarks in the concluding chapter of *The Flowering of New England: 1815–1865*

(New York: E. P. Dutton, 1940), pp. 526–37.

3. This frontier thesis forms the theoretical matrix of Frederick Jackson Turner, *The Frontier in American History* (New York: Henry Holt, 1953). See in particular chap. 1, "The Significance of the Frontier in American History," pp. 1–38.

4. Perry Miller, class lectures in the History of American Literature (Harvard College, 1952).

5. See Robert N. Bellah, *The Broken Covenant: American Civil Religion in Time of Trial* (New York: Seabury Press, 1975), particularly chaps. 1 and 2, "America's Myth of Origin" and "America as a Chosen People," pp. 1–35, 36–60, and his controversial article which first argued for the existence of a civil religion in America, "Civil Religion in America," *Daedalus* 96 (Winter 1967), repr. in Robert N. Bellah, *Beyond Belief: Essays on Religion in a Posttraditional World* (New York: Harper and Row, 1970). Also note his comparative essays in the sociology of culture approaching civil religions, *Varieties of Civil Religion* (San Francisco: Harper and Row, 1980), esp. chap. 1, "Civil Religion: The American Case," pp. 3–26, and coauthor Phillip E. Hammond's "Epilogue: The Civil Religion Proposal," an essentially pessimistic vision of the realization and achievements of the American version of civil religion as an overarching, universally integrative foundation of culture and social life, pp. 200–203.

6. Bellah, *Varieties of Civil Religion*, chap. 1, p. 15.

7. Richard Wightman Fox, *Reinhold Niebuhr: A Biography* (New York: Pantheon Books, 1985). Chapter 1 ("Never Far from the Tree [1892–1913]") describes Niebuhr's beginnings, and "Epilogue: Full of Grace and Grief" examines his life and work in light of his times.

8. See Bellah, *The Broken Covenant*, "Preface," pp. xi ff., and chap. 6, "Birth of New American Myths," pp. 139–63.

9. William Ernest Hocking, *The Coming World Civilization* (New York: Harper and Row, 1956), pp. 118 and 171 ff.

10. Reinhold Niebuhr, *The Nature and Destiny of Man: A Christian Interpretation*, 2 vols. (London: Nisbet, 1942). See esp. vol. 2, chap. 10, sec. 3, "The End and Meaning of History," pp. 309 ff.

11. Paul Sevier Minear, *Eyes of Faith: A Study in the Biblical Point of View*, rev. ed. (St. Louis: Bethany Press, Abbott Books, 1966). See pt. 1, "The Angle of Vision," pp. 33–170 *passim*.

12. Walter Rauschenbusch, *A Theology of the Social Gospel* (New York: MacMillan, 1917).

13. The literature is considerable with volumes of memoirs by the Railroad's organizers and monographs concerning local branches and their operation. For an interesting example of the former, see Levi Coffin, *Reminiscences of Levi Coffin* (1898; repr. New York: New York Times and Arno Press, 1968). In the same series, see the concise history of the Railroad in the state of Pennsylvania (1883) by physician and antislavery activist R. C. Smedley, *History of the Underground Railroad* (New York: Arno Press, 1969). One of the few works to be written by the child of a freed slave is William Still, *The Underground Railroad: A Record of Facts, Authentic Narratives, Letters, Etc.* (Philadelphia: People's Publishing, 1871). Still chaired the Philadelphia branch of the underground railroad.

6. Christianity and the New India

1. For a discussion of the political and cultural significance of civil religion in India, see Leroy S. Rouner's essay, "To Be at Home: Civil Religion as a Common Bond," in *Civil Religion and Political Theology*, ed. Leroy S. Rouner (Notre Dame: University of Notre Dame Press, 1986), chap. 7, esp. pp. 126–27; and Rouner's *Civil Loyalty and the New India*, Hull Papers in Indian Politics, no. 4, Caparo Lecture at the University of Hull (Southall: Shakti Communications, 1989).

2. John Nicol Farquhar, *Modern Religious Movements in India* (Delhi: Munishiram Manoharlal, 1967), esp. chap. 2, "Movements Favoring Vigorous Reform: 1828–1913," pp. 74–81. Also see John Nicol Farquhar, *The Crown of Hinduism* (London: Humphrey Milford, Oxford University Press, 1915), esp. chap. 11, sec. 4, "The Neo-Hindus and the System."

3. Franz Fanon, *The Wretched of the Earth* (New York: Grove Press, 1965).

4. Jawaharlal Nehru, *The Discovery of India* (London: Meridian Books, 1960).

5. Mansour Farhang, "Fundamentalism and Civil Rights in Contemporary Middle Eastern Politics," in *Human Rights and the World's Religions*, ed. Leroy S. Rouner (Notre Dame: University of Notre Dame Press, 1988), pp. 63–75.

6. Nehru, *Discovery of India*, chap. 6, sec. 6, "The Indian Social Structure: The Importance of the Group," p. 242.

7. Ibid., chap. 10, sec. 9, "Religion, Philosophy, and Science," p. 522.

8. Nirad C. Chaudhuri, *The Continent of Circe: Being an Essay on the Peoples of India* (London: Chatto and Windus, 1967), chap. 5, "Janus and His Two Faces," pp. 97–119.

9. Nehru, *Discovery of India*, p. 580.

10. M. M. Thomas, *The Acknowledged Christ of the Indian Renaissance* (London: S.C.M. Press, 1969), esp. chap. 1 regarding the Brahmo Samaj movement, "Rammohan Roy: The Christ of 'the Precepts'," pp. 1–37.

11. See William Ernest Hocking, *Experiment in Education: What We Can Learn from Teaching Germany* ((Chicago: Henry Regnery, 1954), chap. 11, "A German Student Speaks," for a discussion of the meaning and translation of *die tragende Idee*, "the load-lifting idea," p. 147.

12. Rabindranath Tagore, *Towards Universal Man* (Bombay and New Delhi: Asia Publishing House, 1961).

13. Sri Aurobindo, *The Life Divine*, 3d ed. (New York: India Library Society, 1965) pp. 856–99.

14. Chaudhuri, *Continent of Circe*, chap. 5, p. 98. "Between this proclamation of nonviolence in the third century B.C. and its reassertion in the 20th century by Mahatma Gandhi, there is not *one word* of nonviolence in the theory and practice of statecraft by the Hindus."

15. M. K. Gandhi, *An Autobiography or the Story of My Experiments with Truth*, trans. Mahadev Desai (Ahmedabad: Navajivan Publishing House, 1966). See, e.g., pp. 382–83. There are numerous excellent biographies of Gandhi. Significant studies of Gandhi's theory and practice of nonviolence include Judith M.

Brown, *Gandhi and Civil Disobedience: The Mahatma in Indian Politics 1928–34* (Cambridge: Cambridge University Press, 1977); Margaret Chatterjee, *Gandhi's Religious Thought* (Notre Dame: University of Notre Dame Press, 1983); Richard G. Fox, *Gandhian Utopia* (Boston: Beacon Press, 1989); and Rashmi-Sudha Puri, *Gandhi on War and Peace* (New York: Praeger, 1987). See also Ravinder Kumar, *The Making of a Nation: Essays in Indian History and Politics* (New Delhi: Manohar Publications, 1989). The best available book on Gandhi's theory and practice of politics is Bhikhu C. Parekh, *Gandhi's Political Philosophy: A Critical Examination* (Notre Dame: University of Notre Dame Press, 1989).

7. Thinking in a New Way

1. See, e.g., John Herman Randall, Jr., *The Making of the Modern Mind* (Boston: Houghton Mifflin, 1940), esp. chap. 9, "The New Interests of the Modern Age—The World of Naure," pp. 219–24, "The New Method."

2. Harvey Cox, *The Secular City* (New York: Macmillan, 1965).

3. Paul van Buren, *The Secular Meaning of the Gospel* (New York: Macmillan, 1963).

4. The Protestant orthodoxy being renewed in the twentieth century was the Reformation thought of Luther and Calvin. Leading figures in this strongly Germanic movement included Paul Tillich, Reinhold Niebuhr, and H. Richard Niebuhr in this country and Rudolf Bultmann, Oscar Cullman, and Emil Brunner in Europe. The dominant figure, however, was Karl Barth, whose book *The Epistle to the Romans*, trans. Edwyn C. Hoskyns (London: Oxford University Press, 1957), first published in German in 1918, became the definitive statement of "neoorthodox" theology.

5. William Ernest Hocking, *The Coming World Civilization* (New York: Harper, 1956).

6. For the distinction between "technical" and "ontological" reason, see Paul Tillich, *Systematic Theology*, 3 vols. (Chicago: University of Chicago Press, 1951), esp. vol. 1, pt. 1, "Reason and the Quest for Revelation," sec. A, "The Structure of Reason," pt. 1, "The Two Concepts of Reason," pp. 71–105. For various approaches to the same problem, see Charles Davis, *Theology and*

Political Society (Cambridge: At the University Press, 1980); Charles Taylor, *Hegel and Modern Society* (Cambridge: At the University Press, 1979); and the extensive work of Eric Voegelin, including *Anamnesis*, ed. and trans. Gerhardt Niemeyer (Notre Dame: University of Notre Dame Press, 1978), chap. 3, "Reason: The Classic Experience." While the instrumental notion of reason is associated with pragmatism, it is contemporary analytical philosophy which has made the distinction between technical and ontological reason most clearly and has rejected ontological reason most vigorously.

7. See, e.g., "Symposium: The Other Minds Problems," *Journal of Philosophy* 62 (October 1965), and Alvin Plantinga, *God and Other Minds* (Ithaca: Cornell University Press, 1967). For a readable and wide-ranging discussion, in historical context, see Margaret Chatterjee, *Our Knowledge of Other Selves* (Bombay: Asia Publishing House 1963).

8. Speaking in a New Way

1. See Harry A. Wolfson, *The Philosophy of the Church Fathers* (Cambridge, Mass.: Harvard University Press, 1956), chap. 1, " 'The Wisdom of God' and 'The Wisdom of the World'," pt. 7, "The rise of philosophic Christianity among the Fathers of the Church and the reasons for it," pp. 11–14.

2. Charles S. McCoy, *When Gods Change* (Nashville: Abingdon, 1980) puts this theological perspective in context, pp. 39–40, 89–90, 111–13, and 185–86. For a fuller exploration of "story theology" see Robert McAfee Brown, *Theology in a New Key* (Philadelphia: Westminster Press, 1978).

3. Enthusiastic exceptions to this generalization are Charles Hartshorne's books *Anselm's Discovery: A Re-examination of the Ontological Proof of God's Existence* (LaSalle, Ill.: Open Court, 1965), and *The Logic of Perfection* (LaSalle, Ill.: Open Court, 1962). A more cautious exception is Alvin Plantinga, *The Ontological Argument from St. Anselm to Contemporary Philosophers* (Garden City, N.Y.: Anchor Books, 1965).

4. For a perspective on his life's work, see Gabriel Marcel, *Being and Having* (New York: Harper and Row, 1965).

5. See, e.g., H. Richard Niebuhr, "The Nature and Existence of God," in *Motive* (December 1943), p. 13.

6. See Gustavo Gutierrez, *A Theology of Liberation*, ed. and trans. Sr. Caridad Inda and John Eagleson (Maryknoll, N.Y.: Orbis Books, 1973).

7. James H. Cone, *A Black Theology of Liberation* (Philadelphia: J. B. Lippincott, 1970).

8. Rosemary Radford Ruether, *Sexism and God-Talk: Toward a Feminist Theology* (Boston: Beacon Press, 1983).

9. Rudolf Otto, *The Idea of the Holy*, trans. John W. Harvey (New York: Oxford University Press, 1923).

10. While there are more recent studies of the difficulties in reconstructing Jesus' historical life, the great classic is still Albert Schweitzer, *The Quest of the Historical Jesus*, trans. W. Montgomery (London: A. and C. Black, 1931).

11. See, e.g., Karl Barth, *The Humanity of God* (Richmond, Va.: John Knox Press, 1960).

12. See Paul Tillich, *Systematic Theology* (Chicago: University of Chicago Press, 1951), vol. 1, pp. 148–49.

13. Rudolf Bultmann, *Primitive Christianity*, trans. R. H. Fuller (London: Thames and Hudson, 1956).

14. Matt. 26:39.

15. See n. 3, chap. 2.

16. Matt. 8:11–12.

17. See vol. 3.

18. The best contemporary presentation of *Advaita* as a philosophy of life is Eliot Deutsch, *Advaita Vedanta: A Philosophical Reconstruction* (Honolulu: University of Hawaii Press, 1969).

Index